Your Framework

Label your body's framework with the common name of each bone.

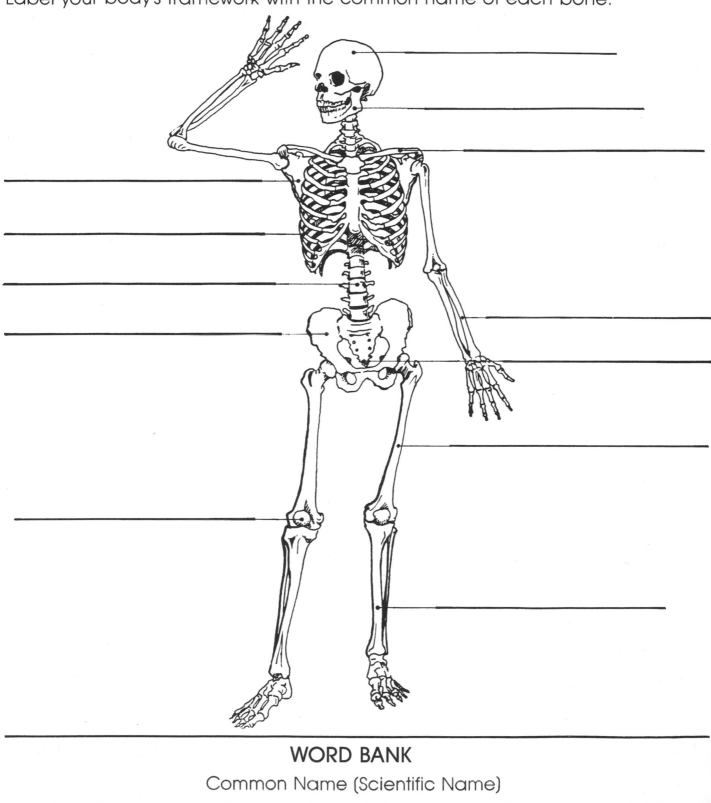

WORD BANK

Common Name (Scientific Name)

skull (cranium)	jawbone (mandible)	collarbone (clavicle)
tailbone (coccyx)	backbone (vertebrae)	shoulder blade (scapula
kneecap (patella)	rib	thighbone (femur)
hipbone (pelvis)	shinbone (tibia)	lower arm bone (ra

3

Your Head Bones

Label these bones that are found in your head and neck.

Name _____

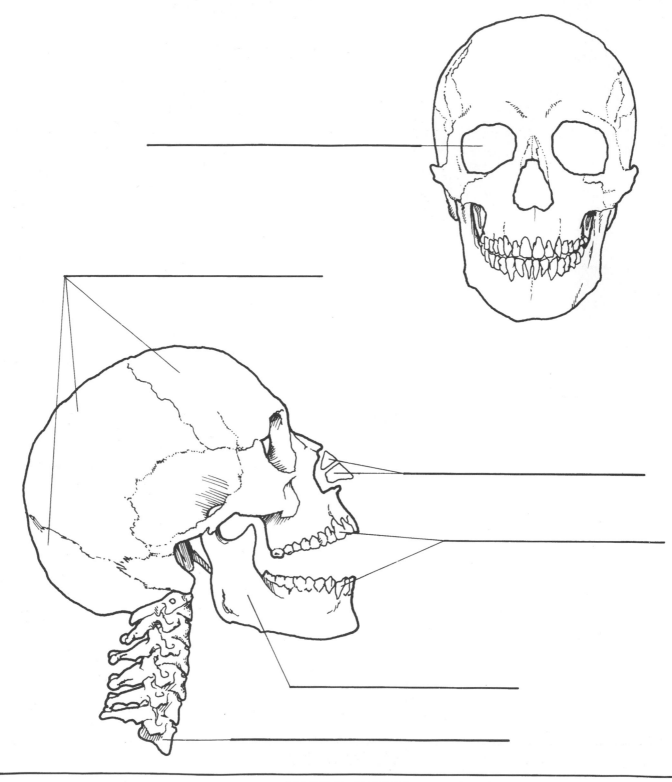

WORD BANK

skull bones   eye socket
jawbone (mandible)   nose cartilage
teeth   vertebrae

Your Body Systems

Name _____

Your body is made of many systems which work together. These systems work in groups. Use the words from the **WORD BANK** to label the different body systems in each group.

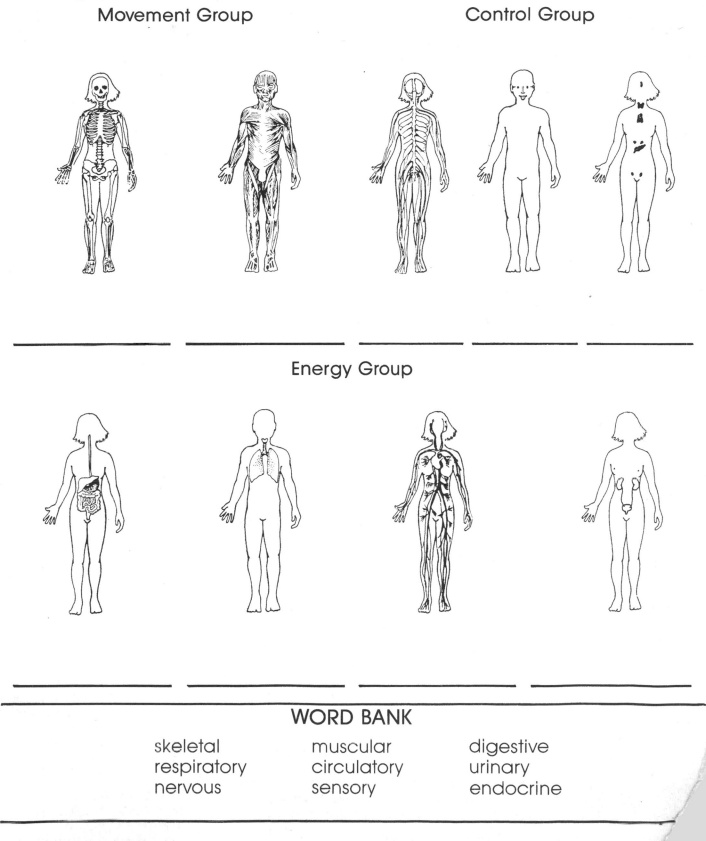

Movement Group

Control Group

Energy Group

WORD BANK

skeletal	muscular	digestive
respiratory	circulatory	urinary
nervous	sensory	endocrine

Your Body Parts

Label all these parts of your body.

Name _____

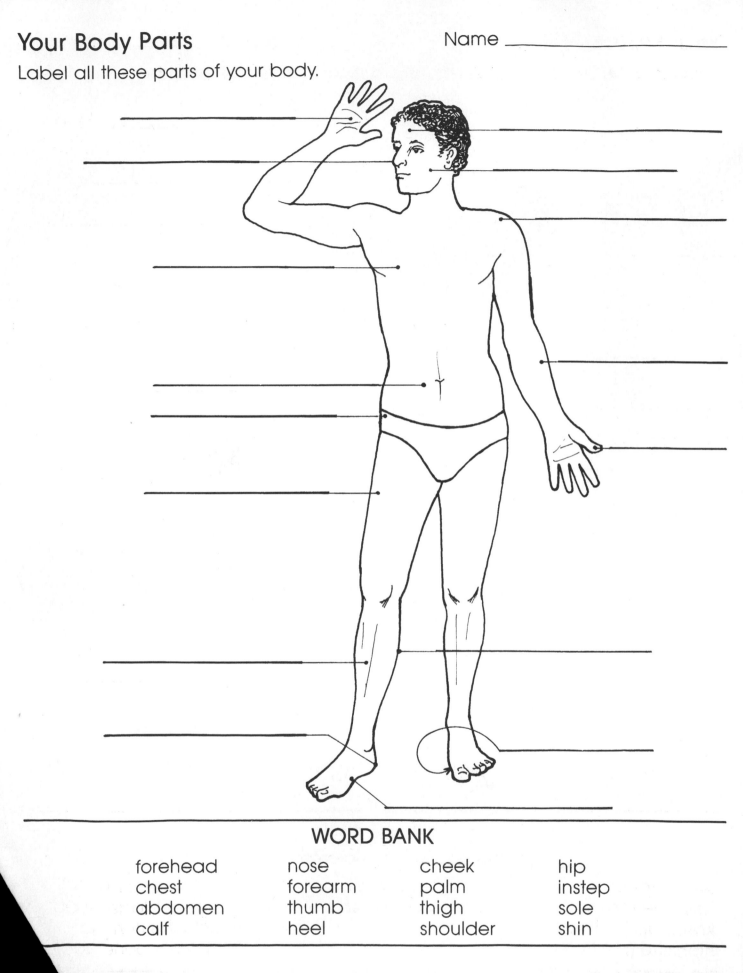

WORD BANK

forehead	nose	cheek	hip
chest	forearm	palm	instep
abdomen	thumb	thigh	sole
calf	heel	shoulder	shin

Your Joints

Label the three kinds of joints pictured below. Also, list examples of where each kind of joint is found.

Kind of Joint	Joint	Man-made Equal	Example

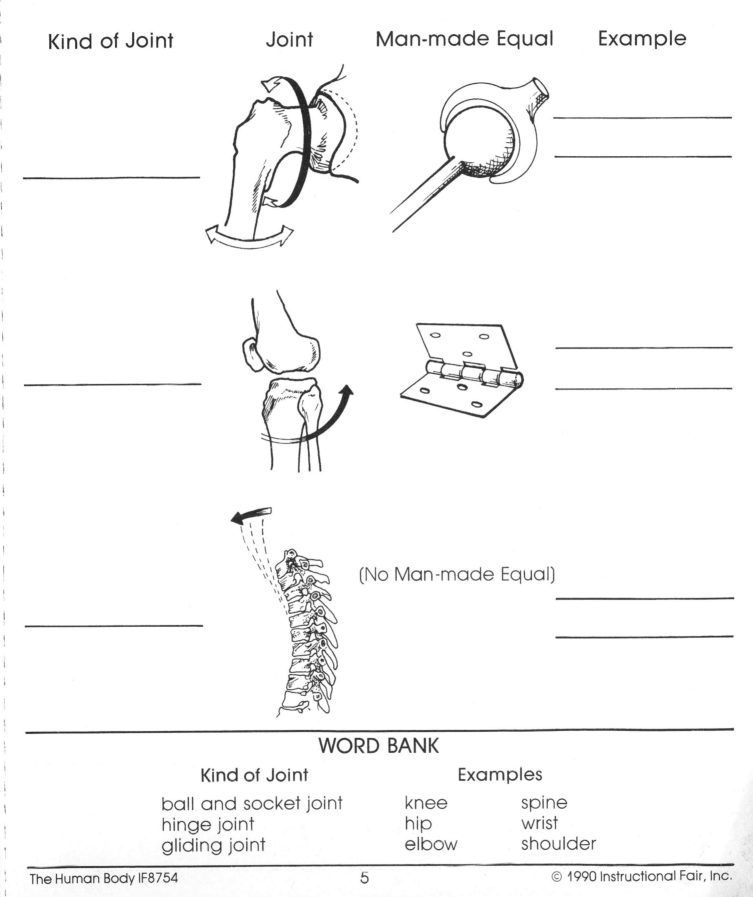

(No Man-made Equal)

_____

WORD BANK

Kind of Joint	Examples	
ball and socket joint	knee	spine
hinge joint	hip	wrist
gliding joint	elbow	shoulder

5

The Leg Bone's Connected to the Hip Bone

Name _____

The place where two or more bones meet is called a **joint**. Joints are either movable or immovable. There are four kinds of movable joints: **hinge, pivot, gliding and ball-and-socket.** Label each joint on the skeleton below.

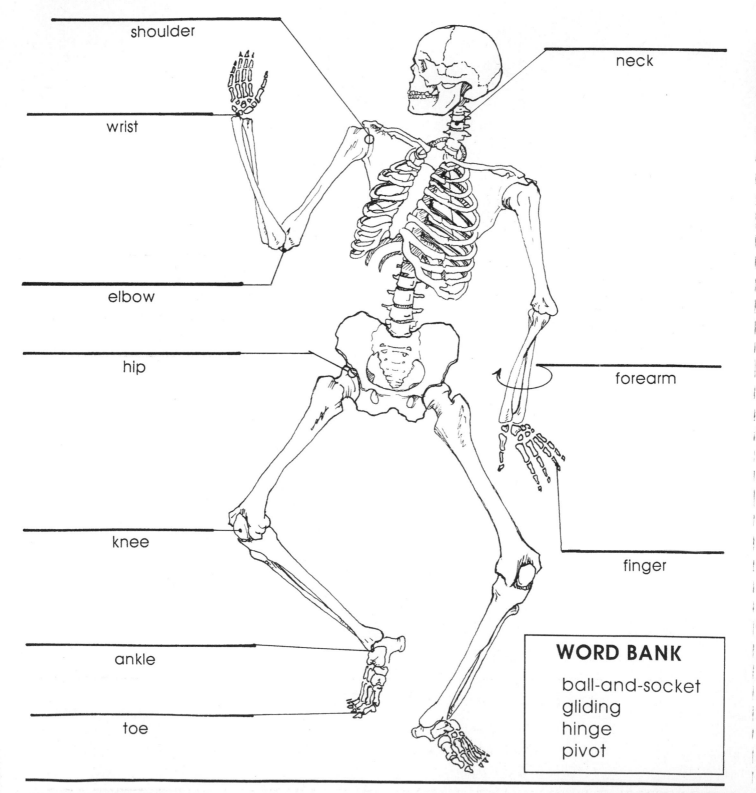

shoulder

neck

wrist

elbow

hip

forearm

knee

finger

ankle

toe

WORD BANK

ball-and-socket
gliding
hinge
pivot

Your Bones

Label the parts of the long bone pictured here.

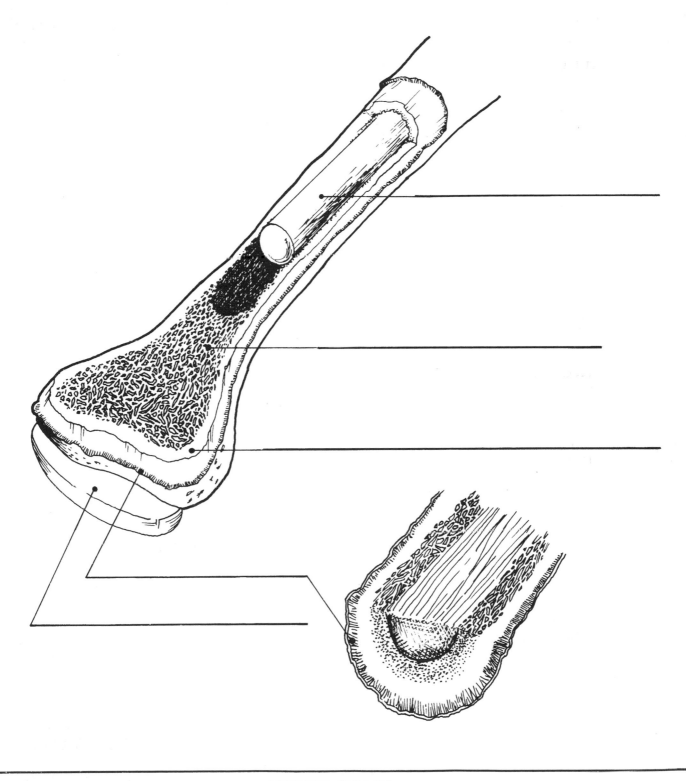

WORD BANK

marrow   periosteum
calcified bone   spongy bone
cartilage

Sticks and Stones May Break Your Bones

Name _____

A break in a bone is called a **fracture**. Some of the common types of fractures are pictured below.

Label the different kinds of fractures.

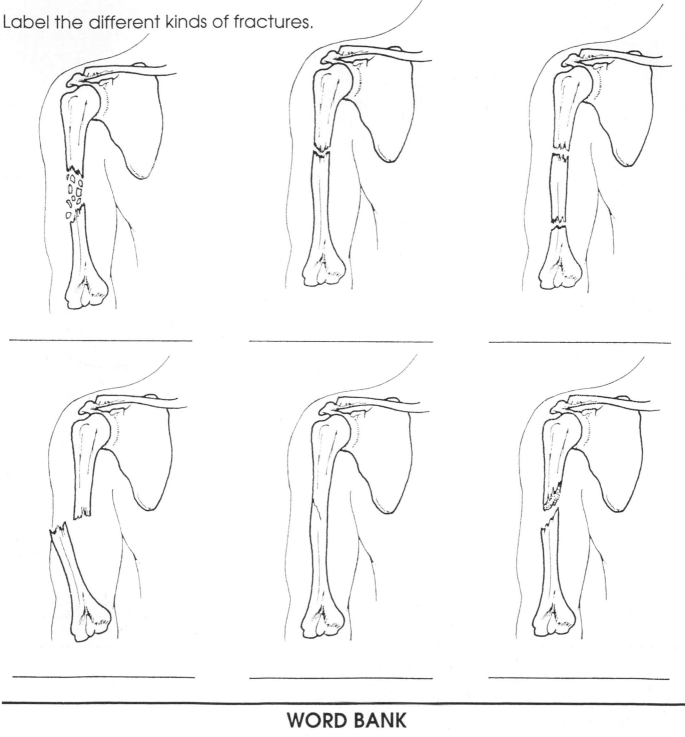

_____   _____   _____

_____   _____   _____

WORD BANK

closed fracture	open fracture	multiple fracture
greenstick fracture	comminuted fracture	spiral fracture

Your Backbone

Name _____

Label the regions of your backbone, or vertebral column.

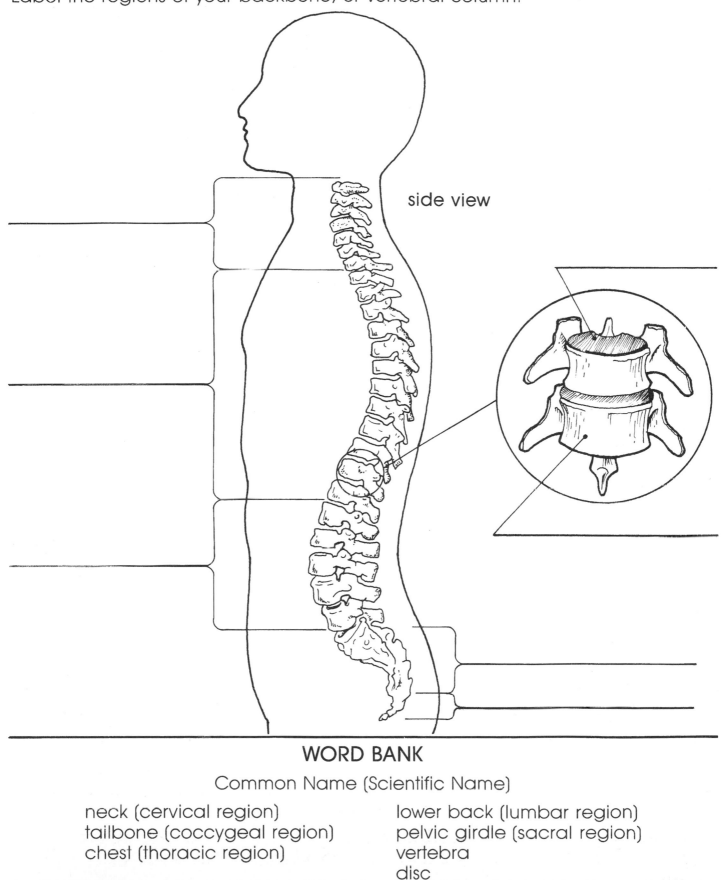

side view

WORD BANK

Common Name (Scientific Name)

neck (cervical region)
tailbone (coccygeal region)
chest (thoracic region)

lower back (lumbar region)
pelvic girdle (sacral region)
vertebra
disc

Your Hands and Feet

Label the bones of the hand and foot.

Name _____

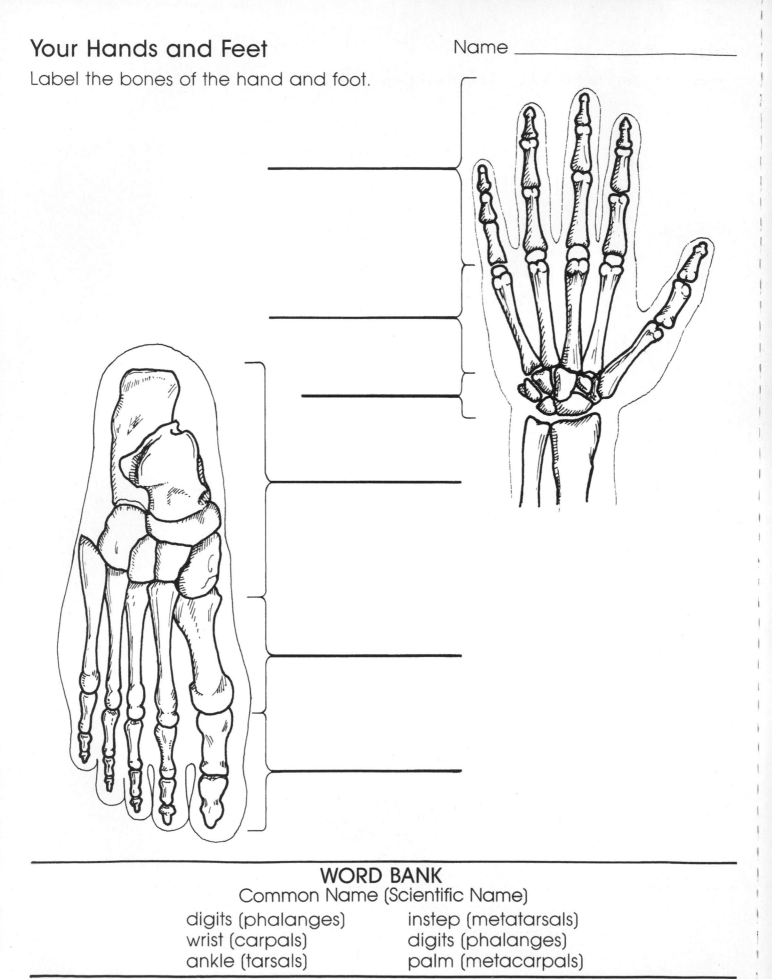

_____

_____

_____

_____

_____

_____

WORD BANK
Common Name (Scientific Name)

digits (phalanges)   instep (metatarsals)

wrist (carpals)   digits (phalanges)

ankle (tarsals)   palm (metacarpals)

Your Leg Bones

Label the different leg bones and regions.

Name _____

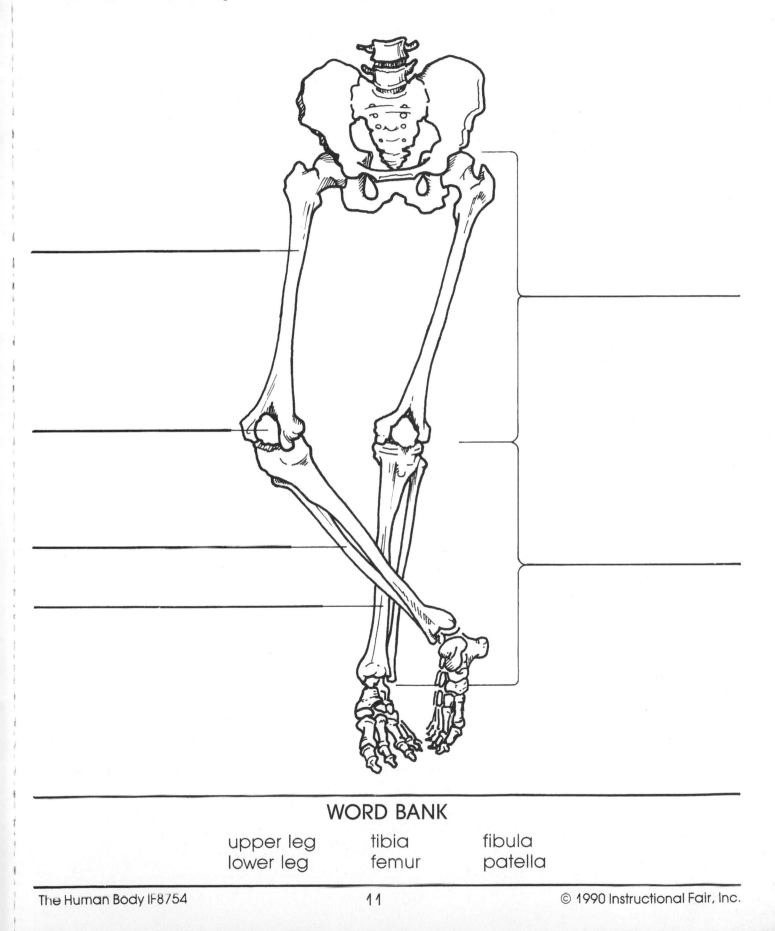

WORD BANK

upper leg   tibia   fibula

lower leg   femur   patella

Your Pelvis

Name _____

The framework of bones that supports the lower part of the abdomen is called the **pelvis**. The male pelvis is heart-shaped and narrow. The female pelvis is much wider and flatter, with a larger central cavity to accomodate a fetus during pregnancy and childbirth.

Label the parts of the pelvis pictured below.

Male Pelvis   **Female Pelvis**

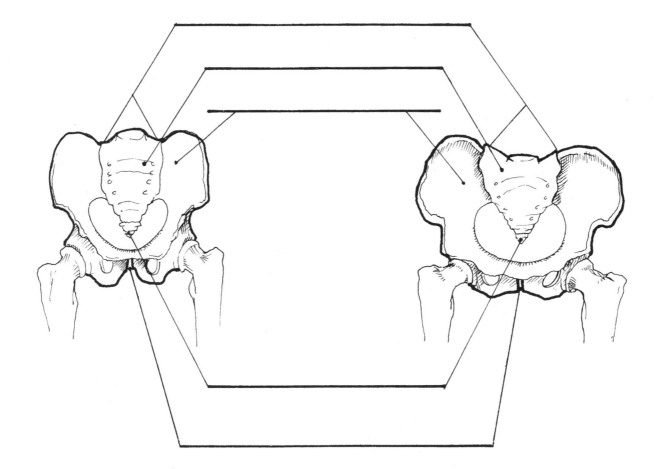

WORD BANK

hipbone	sacrum	coccyx
interpubic joint	sacroiliac joint	

Bones of Your Arm

Label the different arm bones and regions.

Name _____

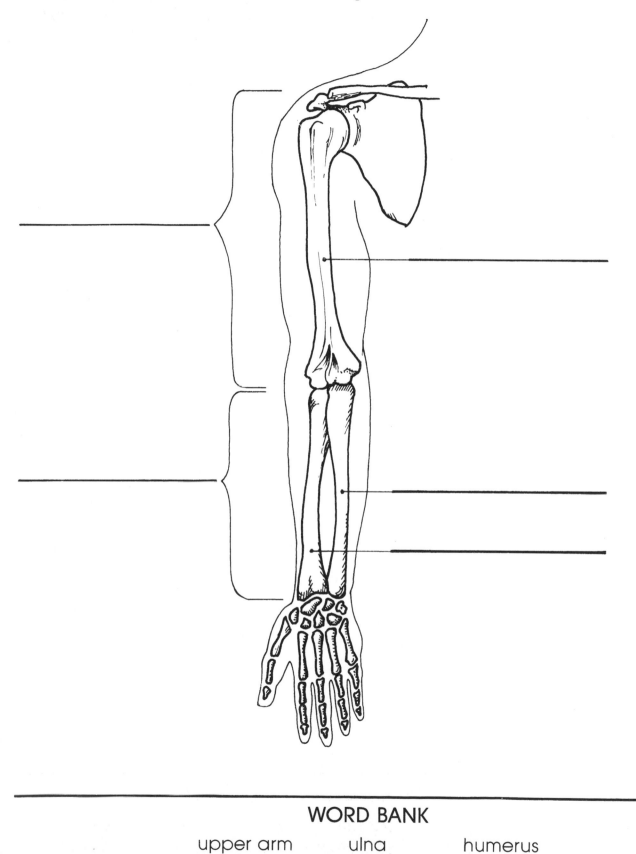

WORD BANK

upper arm   ulna   humerus
lower arm   radius

Inside Your Teeth

Your teeth are made up of a number of layers. Label the layers and outside parts of the tooth below.

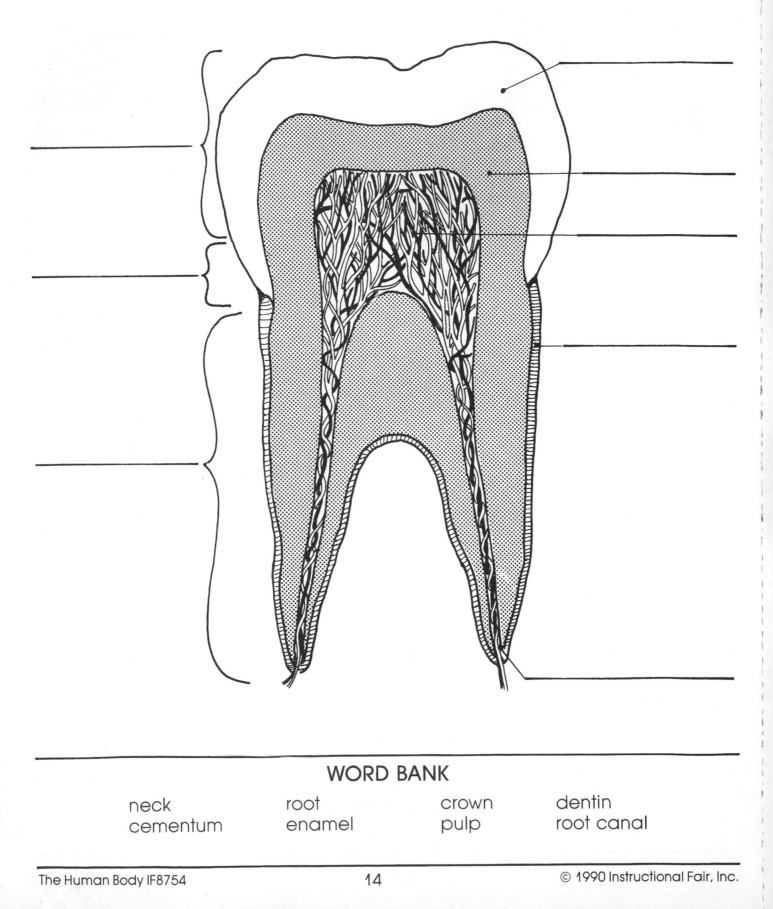

WORD BANK

neck	root	crown	dentin
cementum	enamel	pulp	root canal

A Bit About Bites

Name _____

Each of the pictures on this page illustrates a different **bite**. The bite is the angle at which the upper and lower teeth meet.

Use the Word Bank to label the kind of bite found in each left-hand picture. Then draw a line from the bite on the left side of the page to the corresponding profile on the right side.

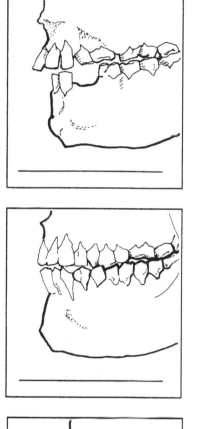

_____

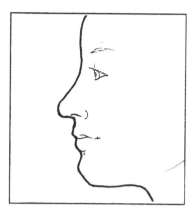

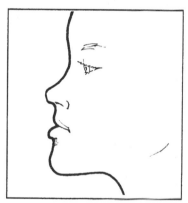

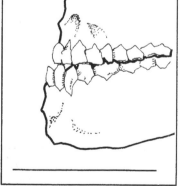

_____

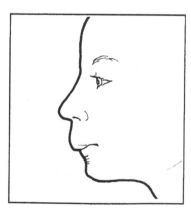

Complete this sentence: "A dentist can correct overbite or underbite by _____

_____."

WORD BANK

overbite	underbite	normal bite

Four Kinds of Teeth

Name _____

You have four kinds of teeth in your mouth. Label the adult teeth pictured below.

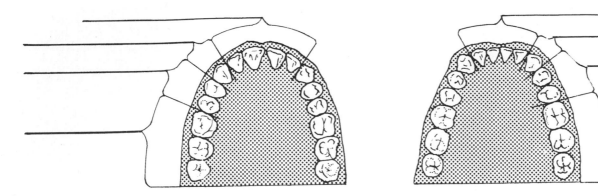
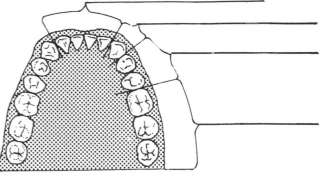

Adult upper   Adult lower

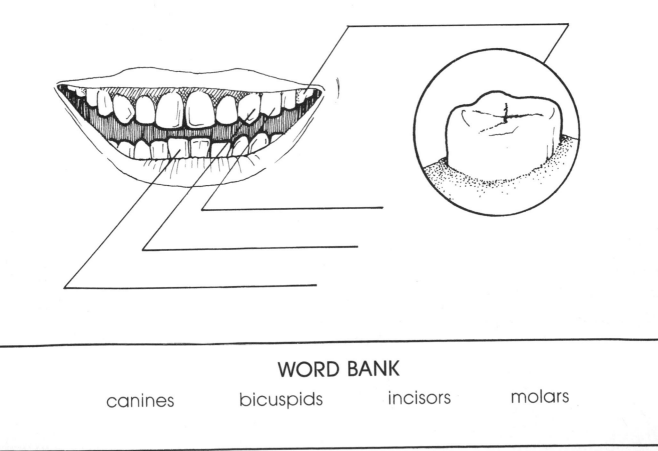

WORD BANK

canines   bicuspids   incisors   molars

Mr. Bones

Cut out Mr. Bones and glue him together. Label Mr. Bones on the lines drawn on the bones using the words below.

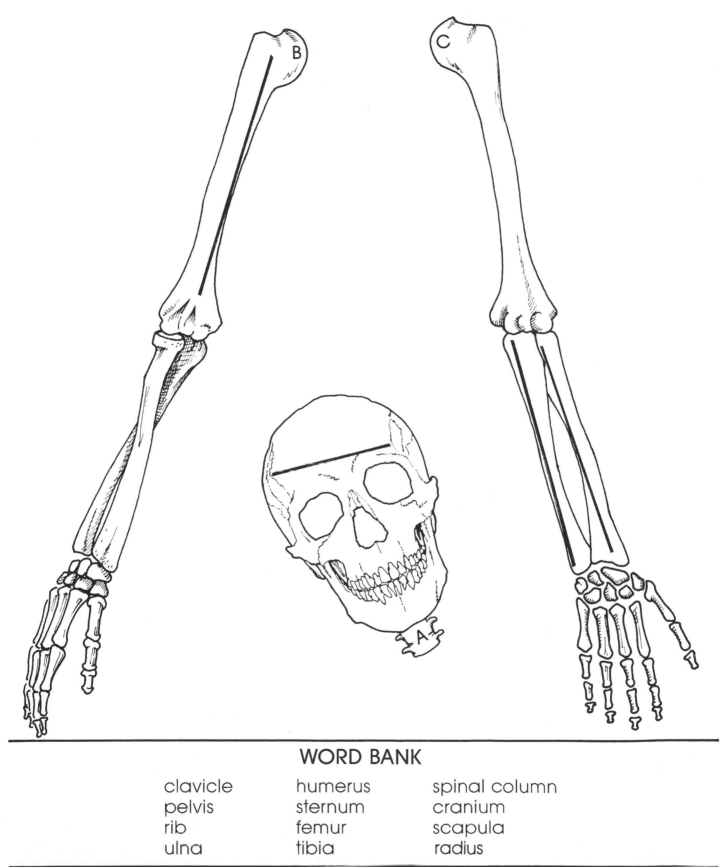

WORD BANK

clavicle	humerus	spinal column
pelvis	sternum	cranium
rib	femur	scapula
ulna	tibia	radius

Name _____

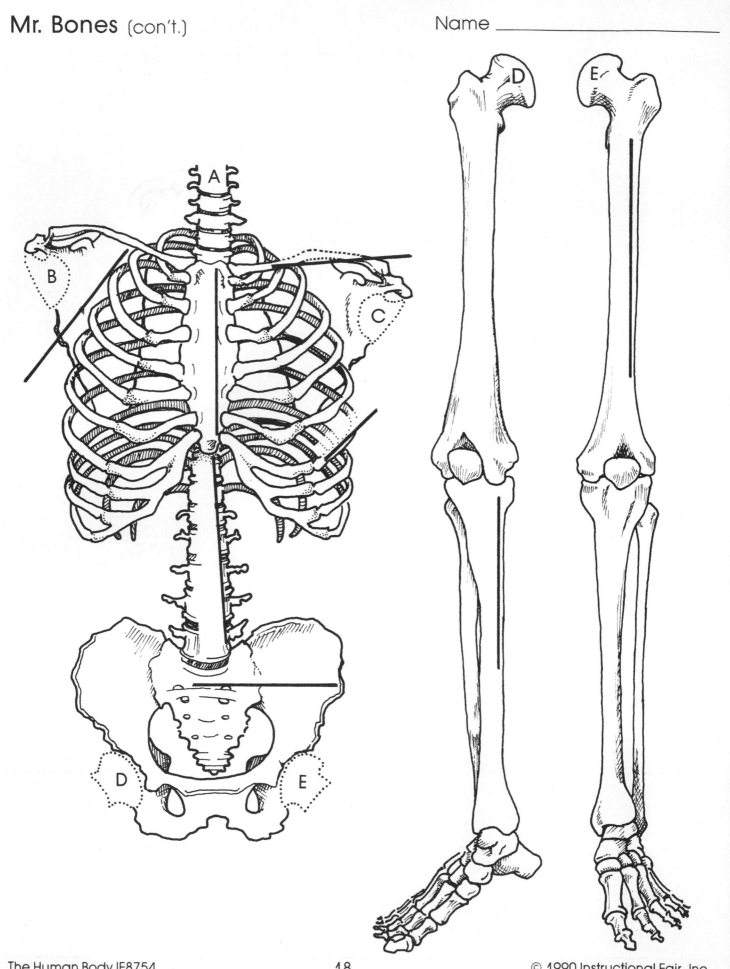

Muscle Man

Name _____

There are hundreds of muscle groups in your body. Label these muscles that appear on the surface of your body.

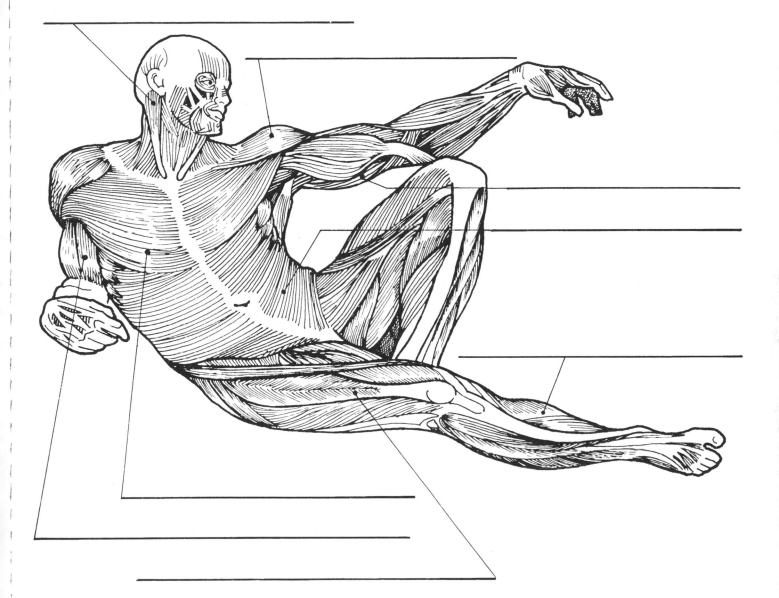

WORD BANK

Common Name (Scientific Name)

chest muscles (pectorals)
calf muscles (gastrocnemius)
biceps
head muscles (sternocleidomastoids)
stomach muscles (inter coastals)

thigh muscles (quadraceps)
shoulder muscles (deltoids)
triceps

Skeletal Muscles

Name _____

Skeletal muscles are attached to the skeleton by means of **tendons**.

Label the parts of the arm pictured below.

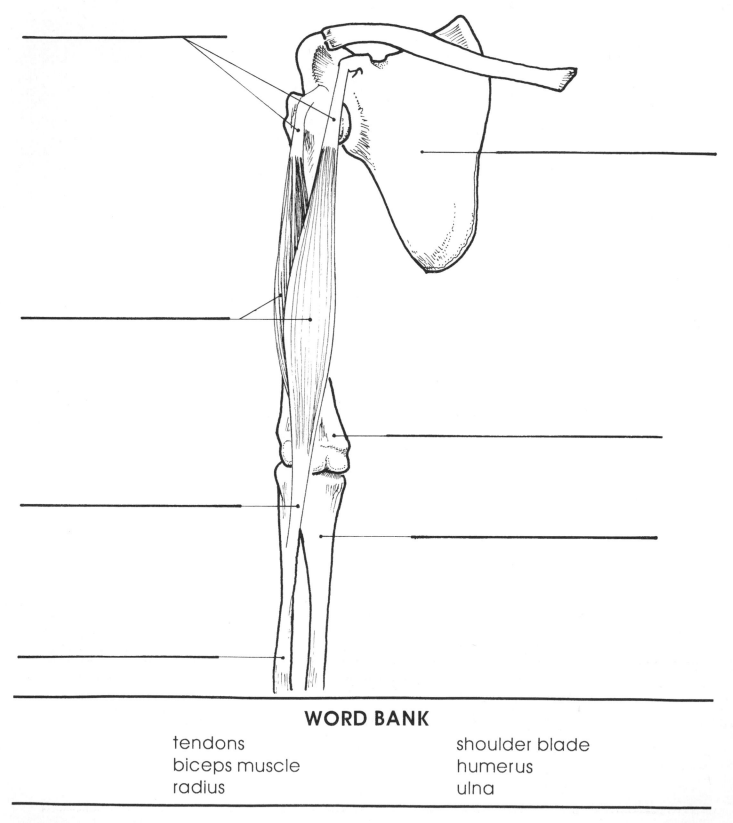

WORD BANK

tendons	shoulder blade
biceps muscle	humerus
radius	ulna

Bones (Skeletal System Review)

Name _____

Use the Word Bank to complete the puzzle.

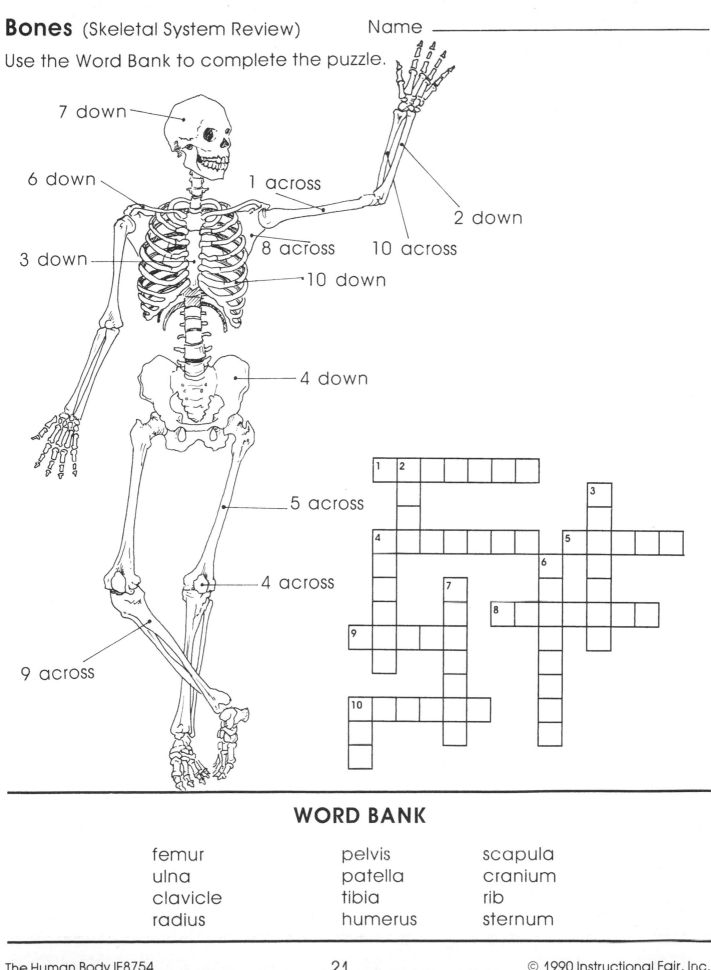

7 down
6 down
1 across
2 down
3 down
8 across
10 across
10 down
4 down
5 across
4 across
9 across

WORD BANK

femur	pelvis	scapula
ulna	patella	cranium
clavicle	tibia	rib
radius	humerus	sternum

Your Muscles

Name _____

Label the three different kinds of muscles in section "A". Give an example of the kind of work they do.

Label the muscle parts in section "B".

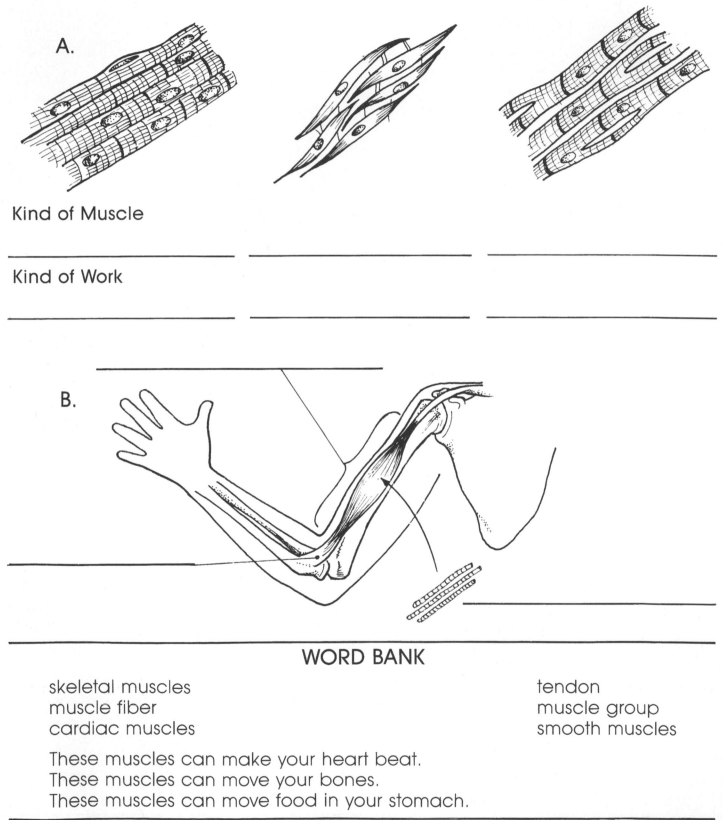

A.

Kind of Muscle

_____   _____   _____

Kind of Work

_____   _____   _____

B.

WORD BANK

skeletal muscles   tendon
muscle fiber   muscle group
cardiac muscles   smooth muscles

These muscles can make your heart beat.
These muscles can move your bones.
These muscles can move food in your stomach.

Working Pairs

The muscles in both your upper arms and upper legs are very much alike.
They both work in pairs to help raise and lower the limbs. Label the parts of
these "working pairs" using the words from the **WORD BANK**.

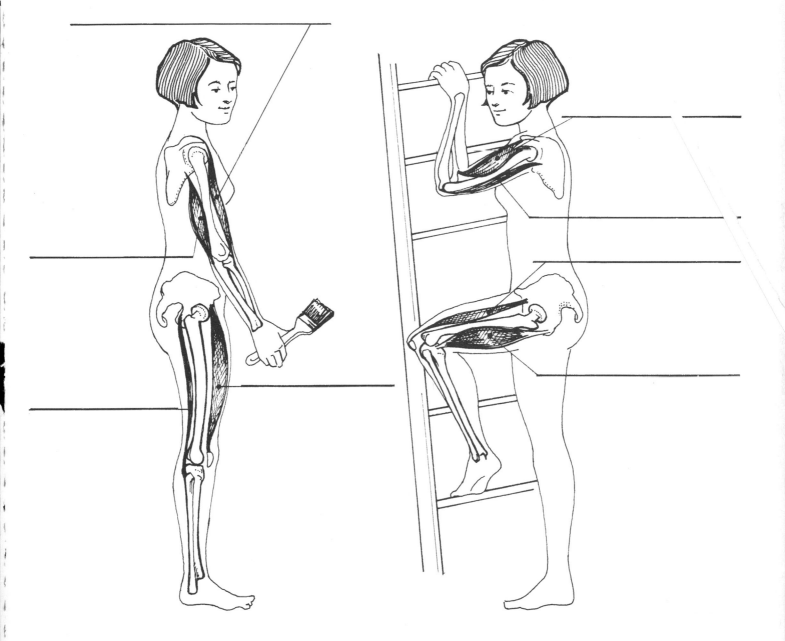

WORD BANK

biceps relaxed	biceps contracted
triceps relaxed	triceps contracted
quadriceps relaxed	quadriceps contracted
hamstring relaxed	hamstring contracted

23

Your Circulatory System

Label the parts of your circulatory system.

Name _____

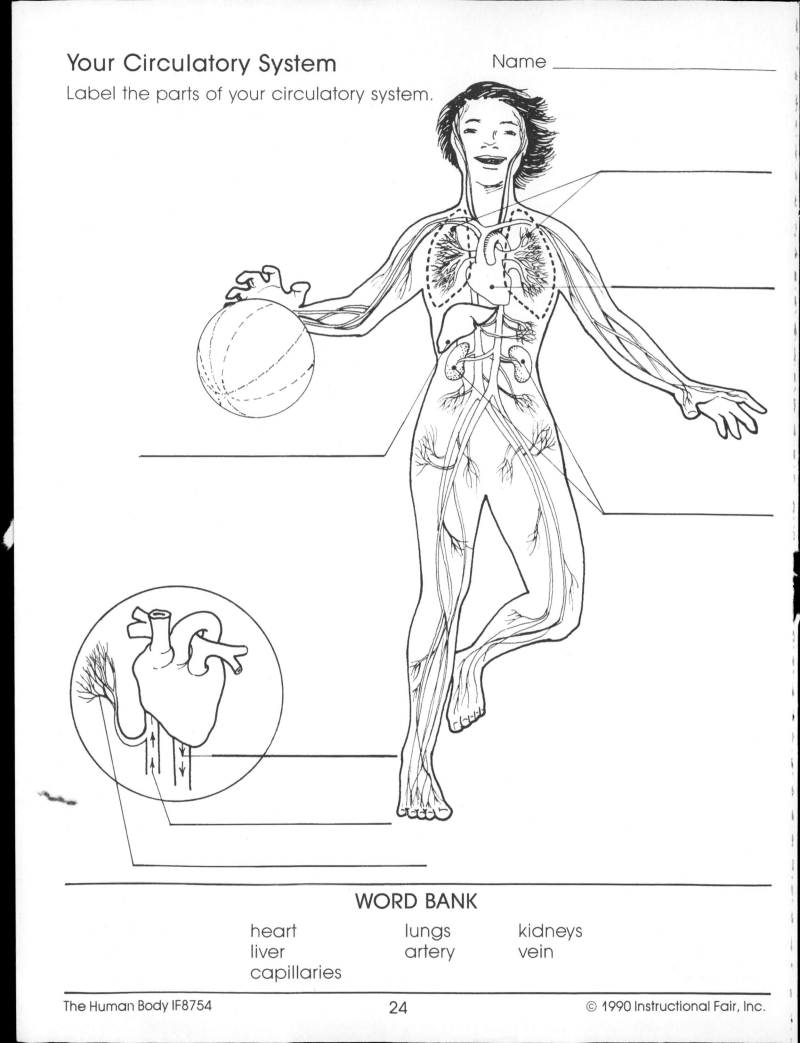

WORD BANK

heart	lungs	kidneys
liver	artery	vein
capillaries		

Veins and Arteries

Name _____

Arteries

Draw red arrows on the arteries showing the flow of blood away from the heart.

Veins

Draw blue arrows on the veins showing the flow of blood back to the heart.

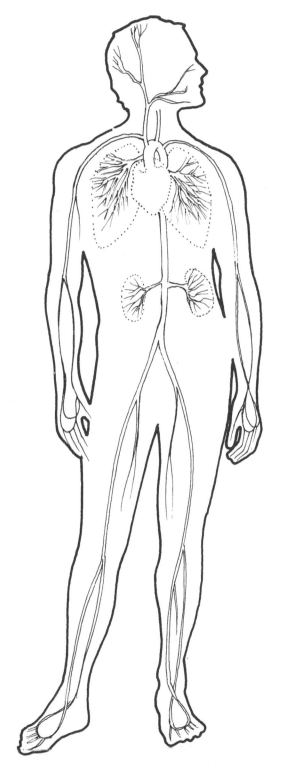

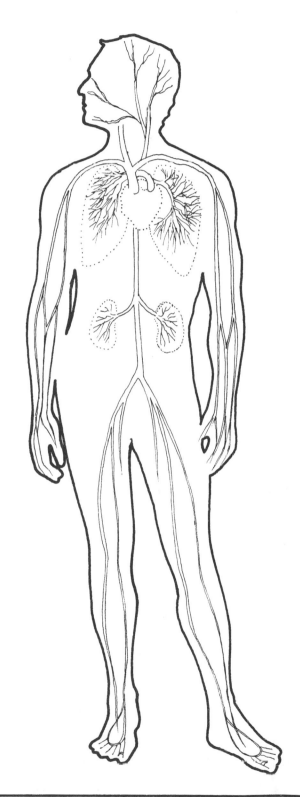

Your Heart

Label the parts of your heart.

Name _____

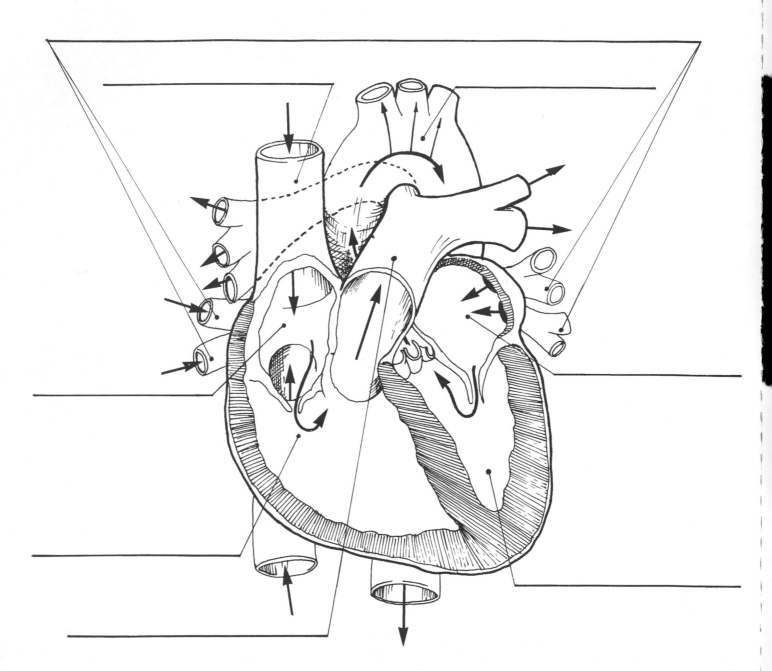

WORD BANK

left atrium	right atrium	vena cava
left ventricle	right ventricle	aorta
pulmonary artery	pulmonary veins	

Your Heart, the Blood Pump

Name _____

Your heart has the job of pumping blood to the many parts of your body. Label the parts of the heart and the location of the flow of blood.

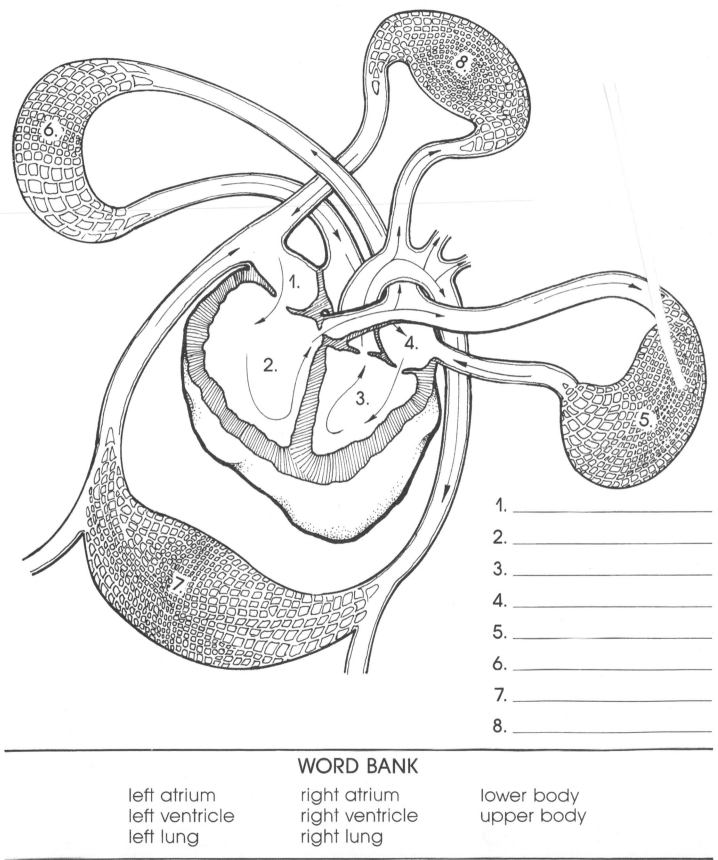

1. _____
2. _____
3. _____
4. _____
5. _____
6. _____
7. _____
8. _____

WORD BANK

left atrium	right atrium	lower body
left ventricle	right ventricle	upper body
left lung	right lung	

Lub – Dub, Lub – Dub
(Circulatory System Review)

Name _____

Use the Word Bank
to complete the puzzle.

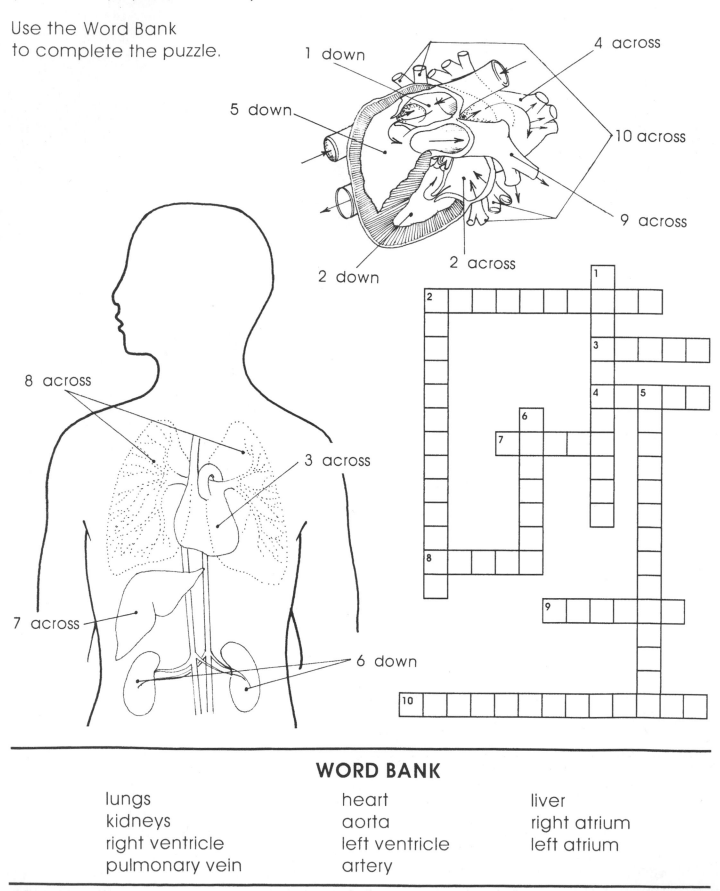

1 down
5 down
4 across
10 across
9 across
2 across
2 down
8 across
3 across
7 across
6 down

WORD BANK

lungs	heart	liver
kidneys	aorta	right atrium
right ventricle	left ventricle	left atrium
pulmonary vein	artery	

Your Respiratory System

Label the parts of your respiratory system.

Name _____

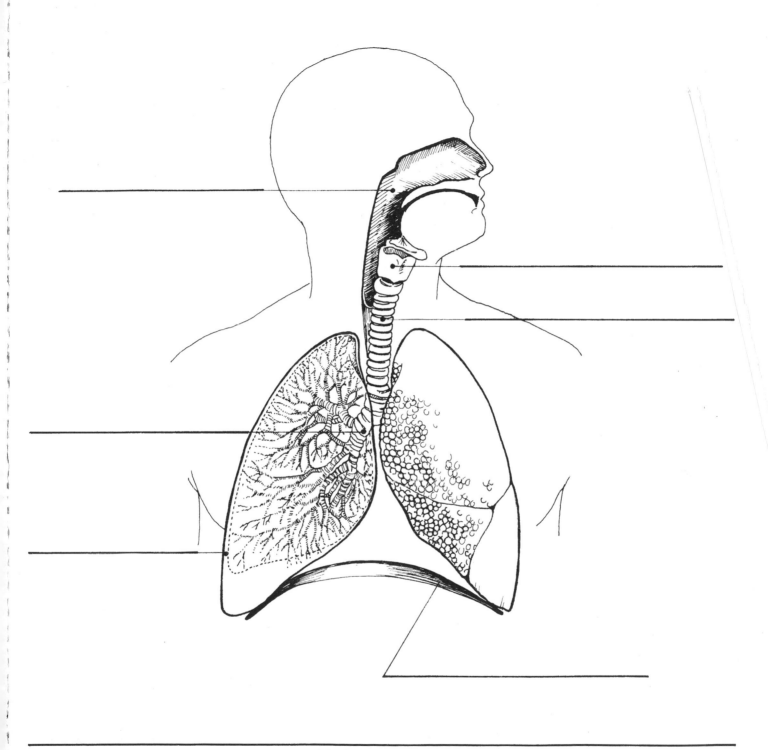

WORD BANK

Common Name (Scientific Name)

throat (pharynx)   voice box (larynx)
windpipe (trachea)   lung cover (pleura)
bronchial tube   diaphragm

Your Lungs

Label the parts of your lungs.

Name _____

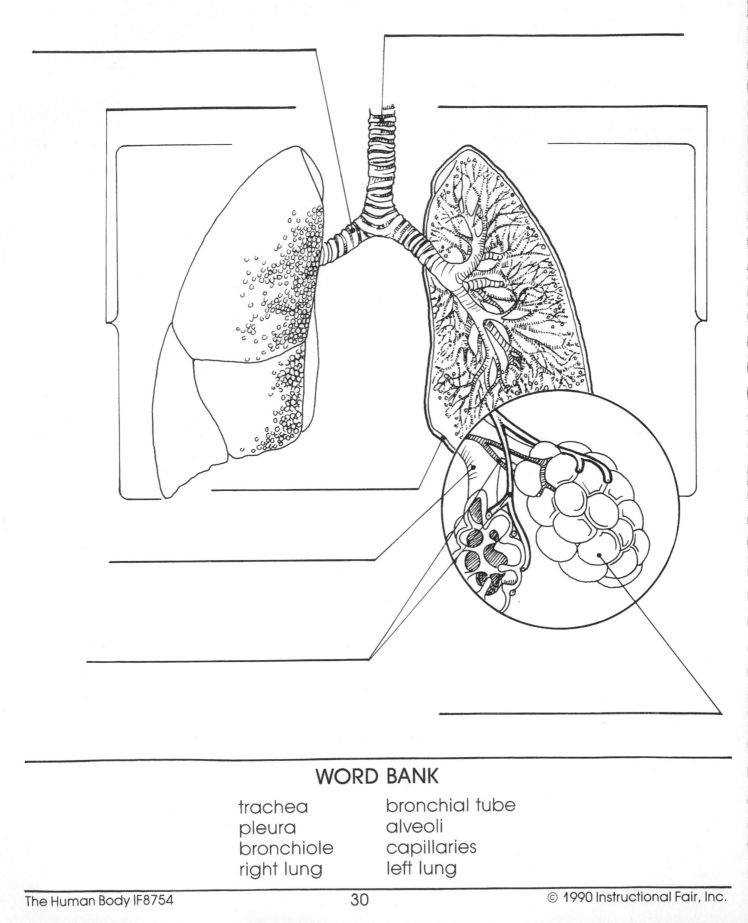

WORD BANK

trachea   bronchial tube
pleura   alveoli
bronchiole   capillaries
right lung   left lung

Breathe In! Breathe Out!

Name _____

You breathe in and breathe out almost 20,000 times each day! Label these two pictures either **INHALE** (breathe in) or **EXHALE** (breathe out). Label the other parts of your breathing system using the words from the **WORD BANK**.

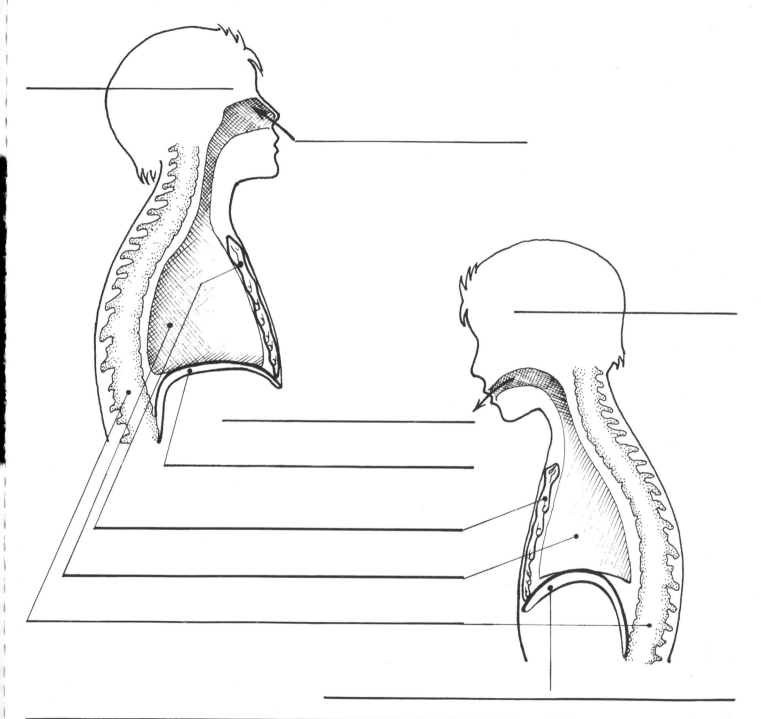

WORD BANK

contracted diaphragm

lung

carbon dioxide

spine

relaxed diaphragm

oxygen

breastbone

Huff – Puff
(Respiratory System Review)

Name _____

Use the Word Bank to complete the puzzle.

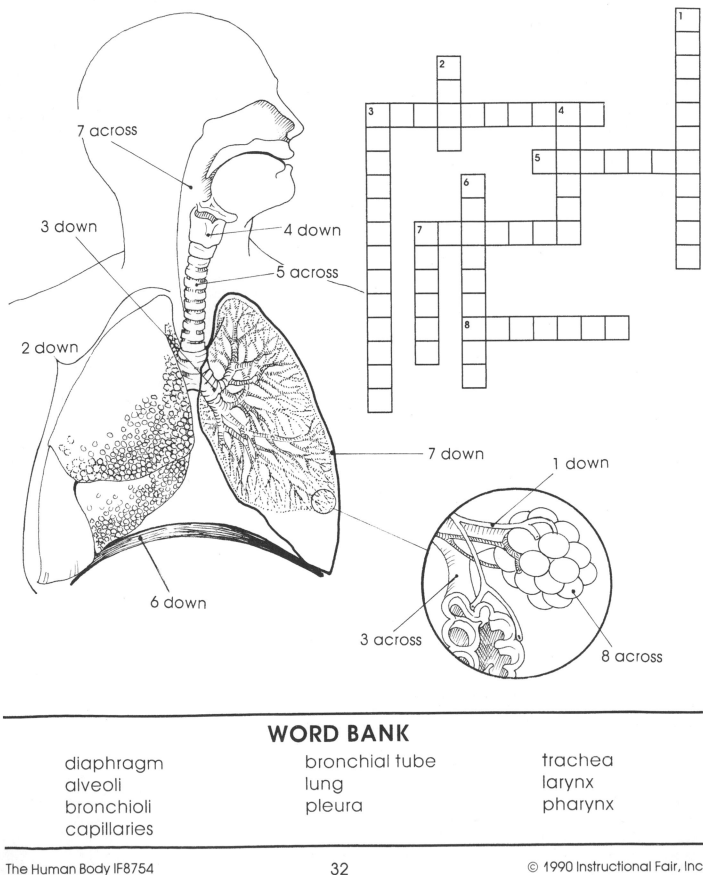

7 across

3 down

2 down

4 down

5 across

7 down

1 down

6 down

3 across

8 across

WORD BANK

diaphragm	bronchial tube	trachea
alveoli	lung	larynx
bronchioli	pleura	pharynx
capillaries		

Your Digestive System

Label the parts of your digestive system.

Name _____

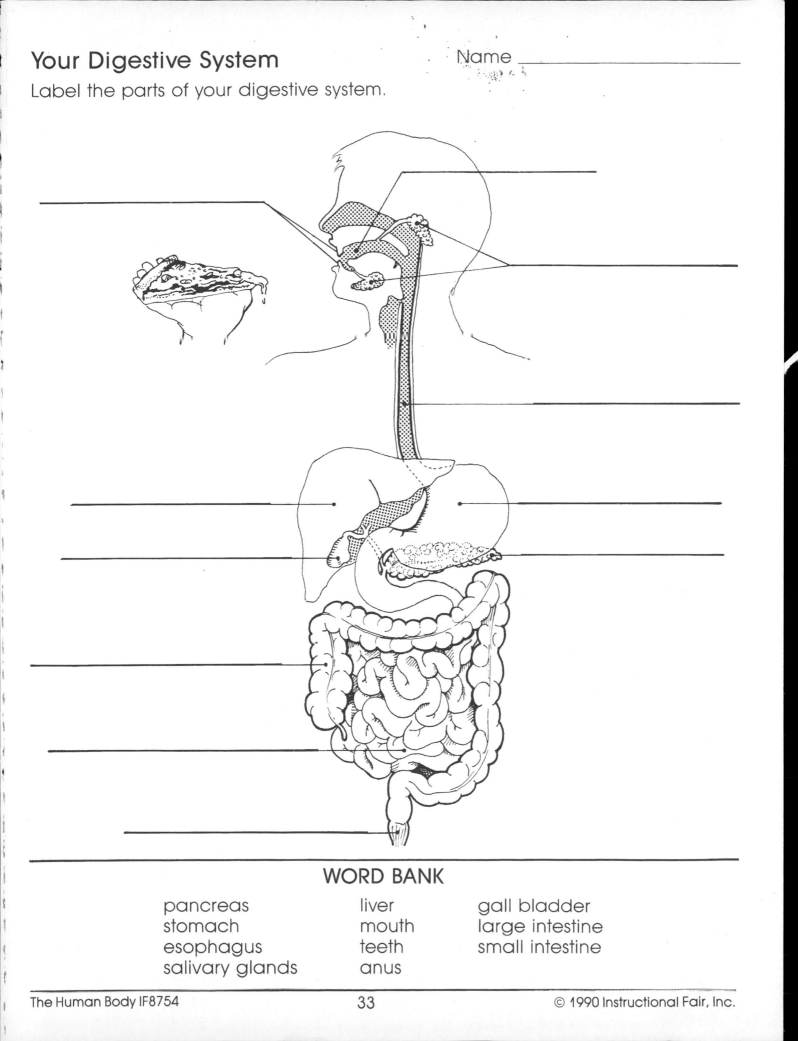

WORD BANK

pancreas	liver	gall bladder
stomach	mouth	large intestine
esophagus	teeth	small intestine
salivary glands	anus	

The Alimentary Canal

Name _____

The main part of the digestive system is the **alimentary canal**, a tube which starts at the mouth, and travels through the body ending at the anus.
Label the parts of the alimentary canal.

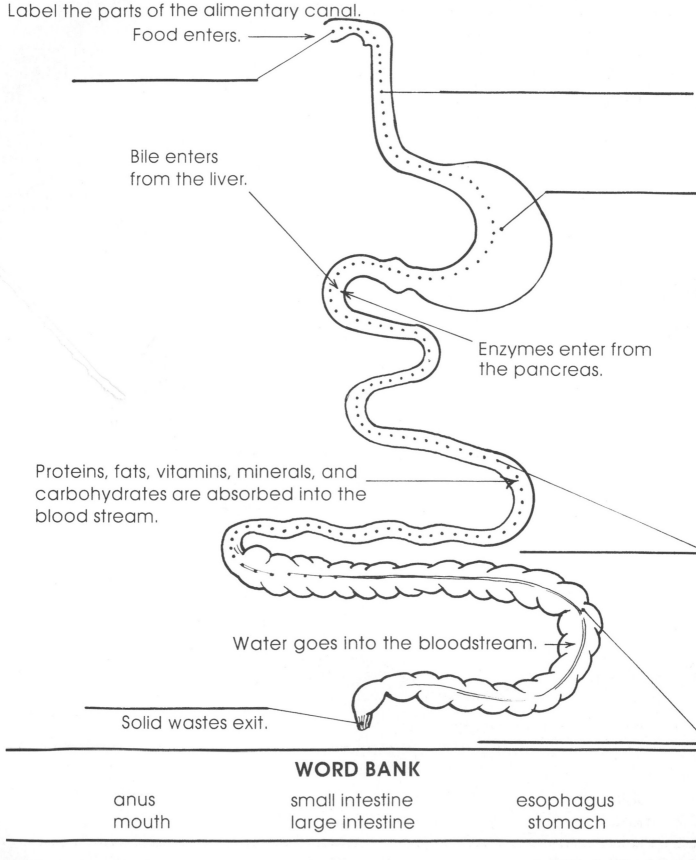

Food enters. ⟶

_____

Bile enters
from the liver.

Enzymes enter from
the pancreas.

Proteins, fats, vitamins, minerals, and
carbohydrates are absorbed into the
blood stream.

Water goes into the bloodstream. ⟶

Solid wastes exit.

WORD BANK

anus	small intestine	esophagus
mouth	large intestine	stomach

The Stomach

The **stomach** is the widest part of the alimentary canal. The stomach has three layers of muscles which allow it to contract in different directions. The contracting motion mashes food and mixes it with digestive juices.

Label the parts of the stomach and the tubes leading into and out of the stomach.

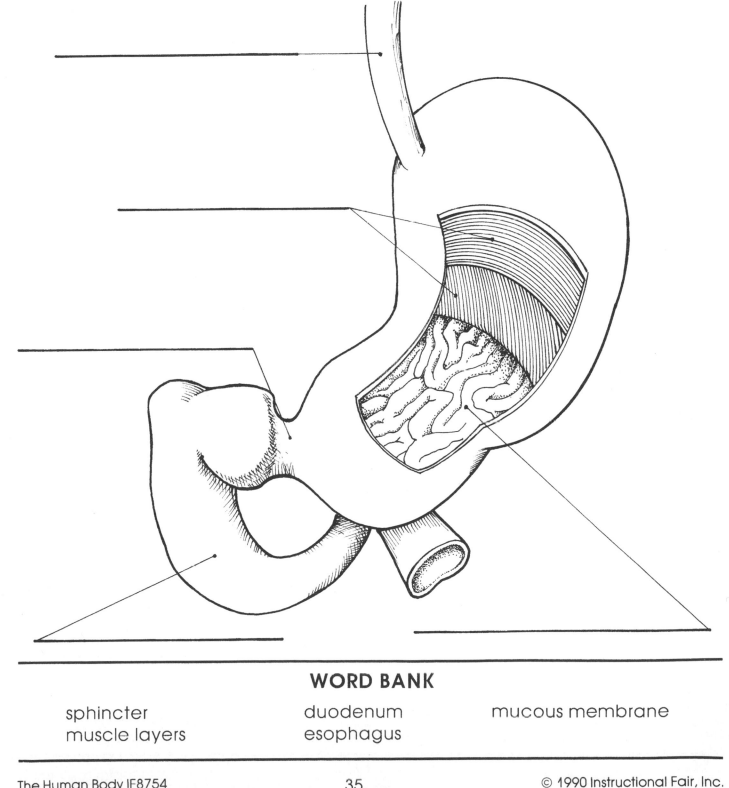

WORD BANK

sphincter	duodenum	mucous membrane
muscle layers	esophagus	

Digestion in the Mouth

Name _____

Label the parts of the digestive system located in and around the mouth.

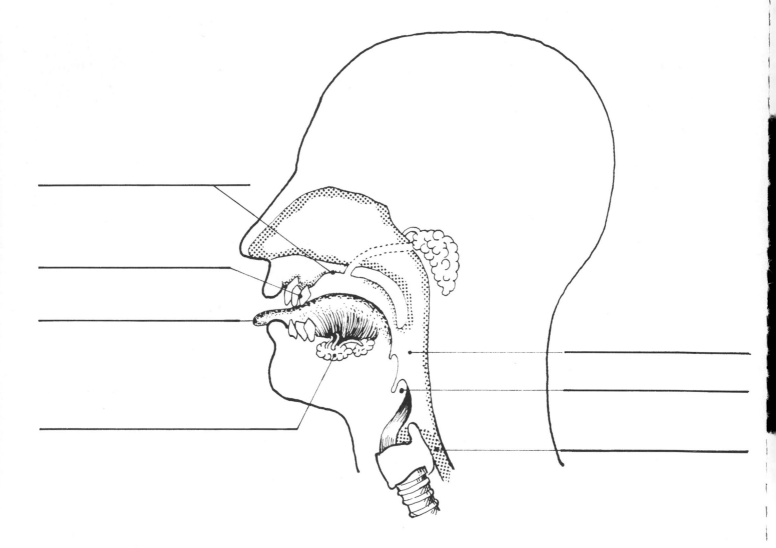

WORD BANK

teeth	tongue	palate
epiglottis	esophagus	salivary glands
pharynx		

     36   © 1990 Instructional Fair, Inc.

Pancreas, Liver, Gall Bladder
Digestion Helpers

Name _____

Label these organs that aid in the digestion of the food you eat.

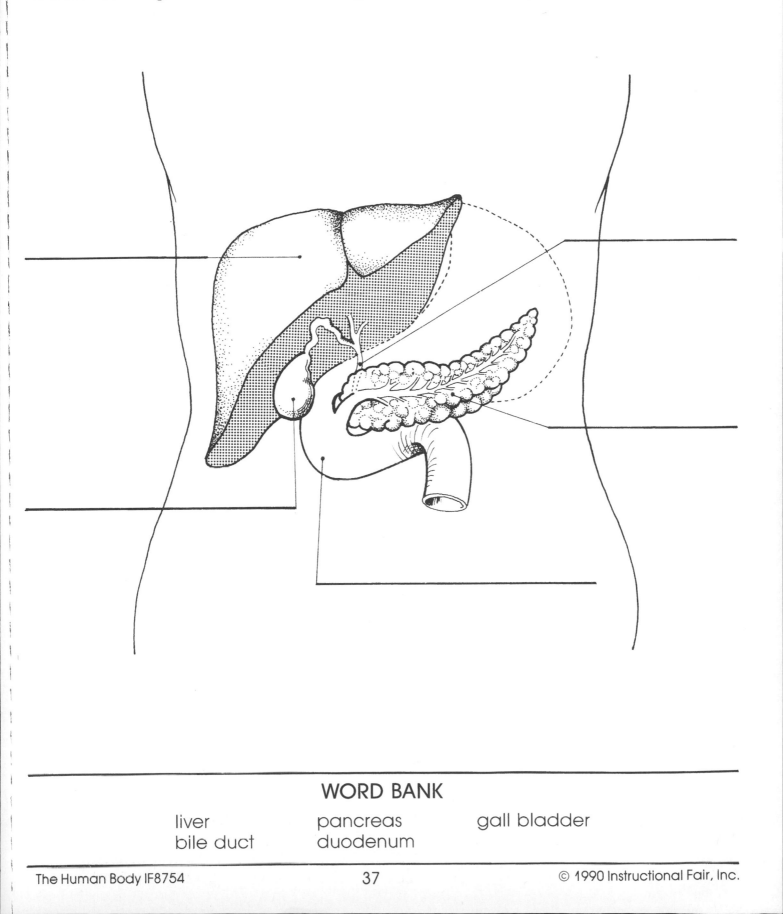

WORD BANK

liver	pancreas	gall bladder
bile duct	duodenum	

Gulp, Gulp

(Digestive System Review)

Name _____

Use the Word Bank to complete the puzzle.

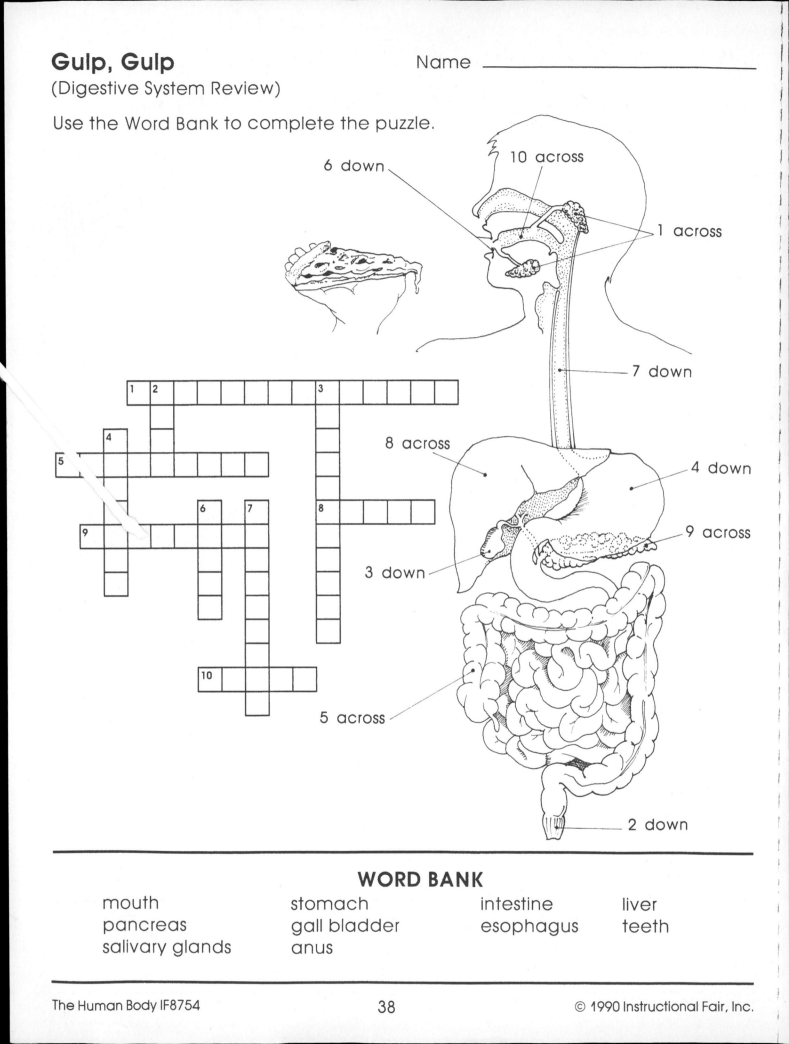

6 down

10 across

1 across

7 down

8 across

4 down

9 across

3 down

5 across

2 down

WORD BANK

mouth	stomach	intestine	liver
pancreas	gall bladder	esophagus	teeth
salivary glands	anus		

Let's Look in Your Mouth!

Name _____

What do you see when you open your mouth in front of a mirror?
Label the different parts.

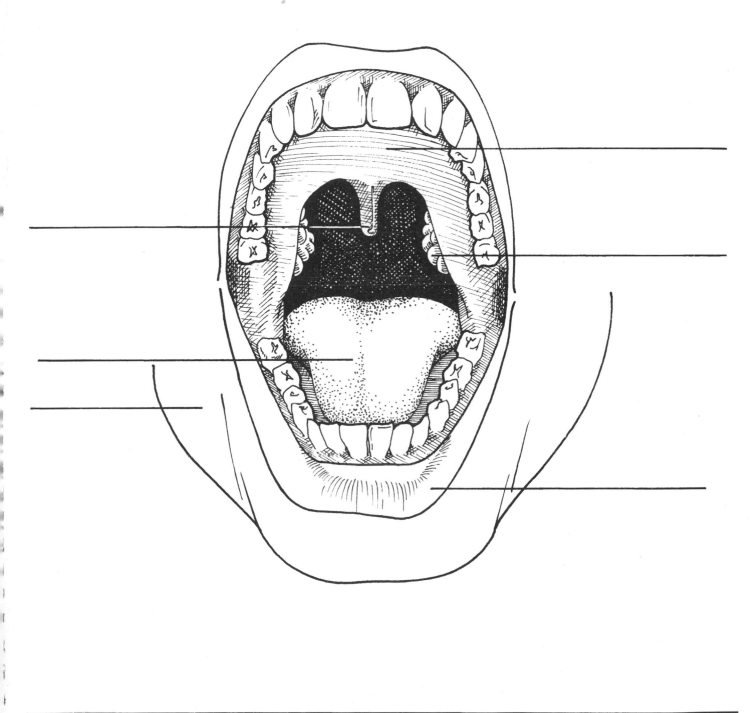

WORD BANK

tongue	uvula	cheek
lip	tonsils	palate

39

Your Long Food Tube

Name _____

Your digestive system is like a big tube that carries the food you eat through your body. Label each part with words from the **WORD BANK**. Draw a line from the description to the part of the digestive system.

"I'm the entrance to the food tube. I chew the food up well."

"I store the food for 3–4 hours while digestion is occurring. My churning breaks down protein."

"Waste exits from my opening."

"Final digestion takes place in my 20-foot-long tube."

"I'm a muscular tube that squeezes the food down to the stomach."

"I store the solid waste and remove the water."

"I'm the first part of the small intestine. Food enters me after it leaves the stomach. "

"We make chemicals to help break down the food."

WORD BANK

small intestine	large intestine	stomach
anus	duodenum	liver, pancreas
esophagus	mouth	gall bladder

Blood Scrubbers

Name _____

Label the different parts of your body's urinary system.

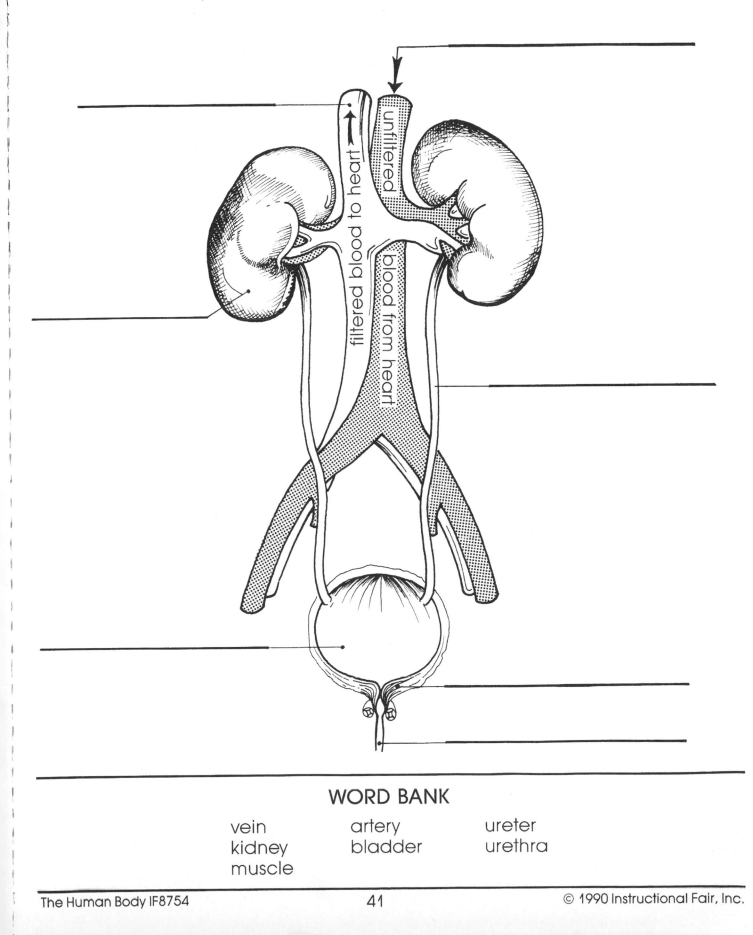

WORD BANK

vein	artery	ureter
kidney	bladder	urethra
muscle		

Waste Removal

Name _____

The important job of removing bodily wastes is performed by the skin and the organs of the urinary and respiratory systems.

Label the **excretory** organs.

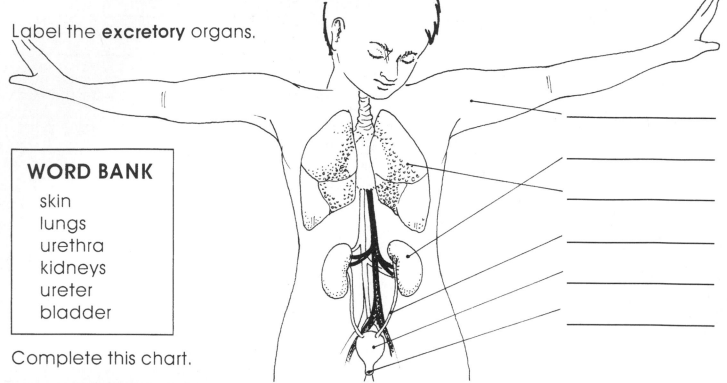

WORD BANK

skin
lungs
urethra
kidneys
ureter
bladder

Complete this chart.

Function	Excretory Organs			
	kidneys	lungs	skin	bladder
removes water				
brings oxygen to blood				
removes salt				
stores urine				
removes carbon dioxide				
produces urine				
removes body heat				

Your Central Nervous System

Name _____

Label the parts of your central nervous system.

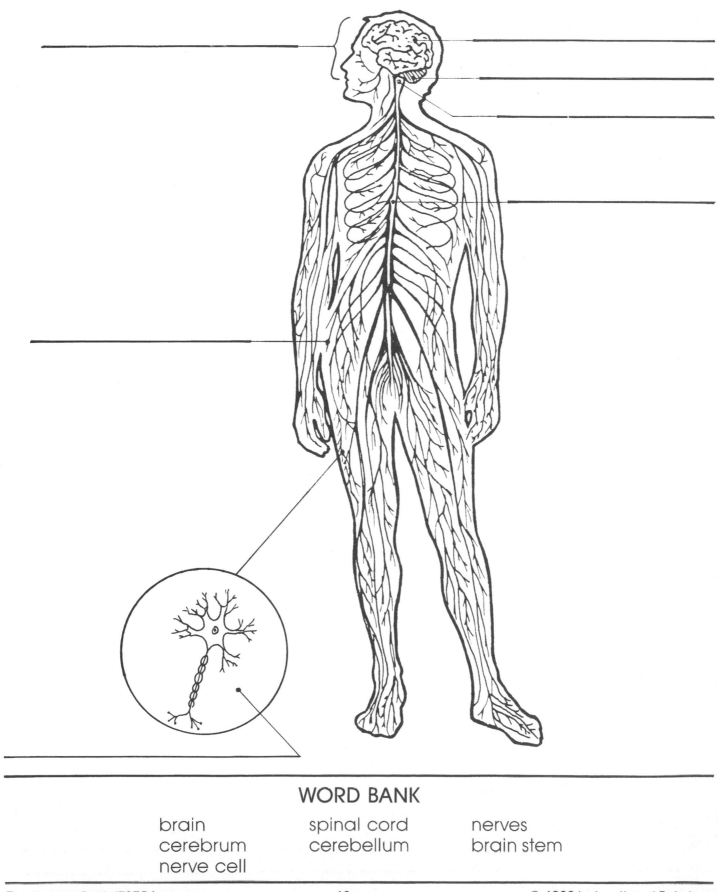

WORD BANK

brain	spinal cord	nerves
cerebrum	cerebellum	brain stem
nerve cell		

Neurons

Name _____

Label the parts of a neuron.

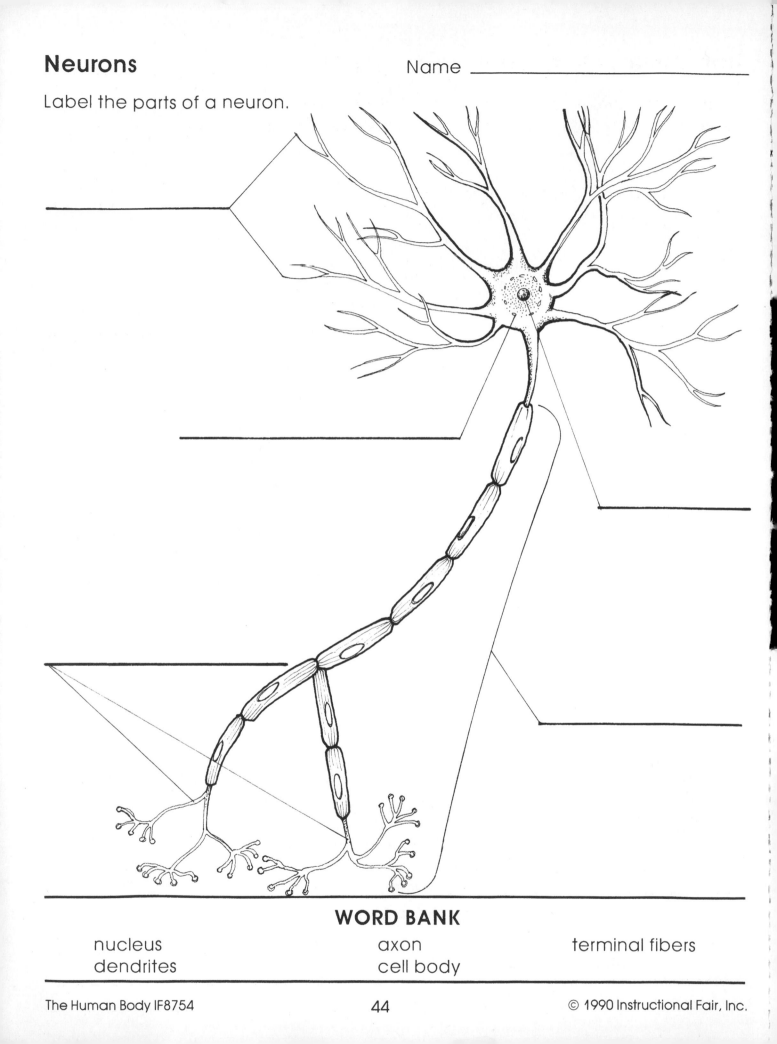

WORD BANK

nucleus   axon   terminal fibers
dendrites   cell body

Transmitters of Impulses

Name _____

Neurons act as "go betweens" in the sending and receiving of impulses within the nervous system. The drawings below illustrate how impulses pass from one neuron to another.

Label the parts of the enlarged illustration.

Synapse

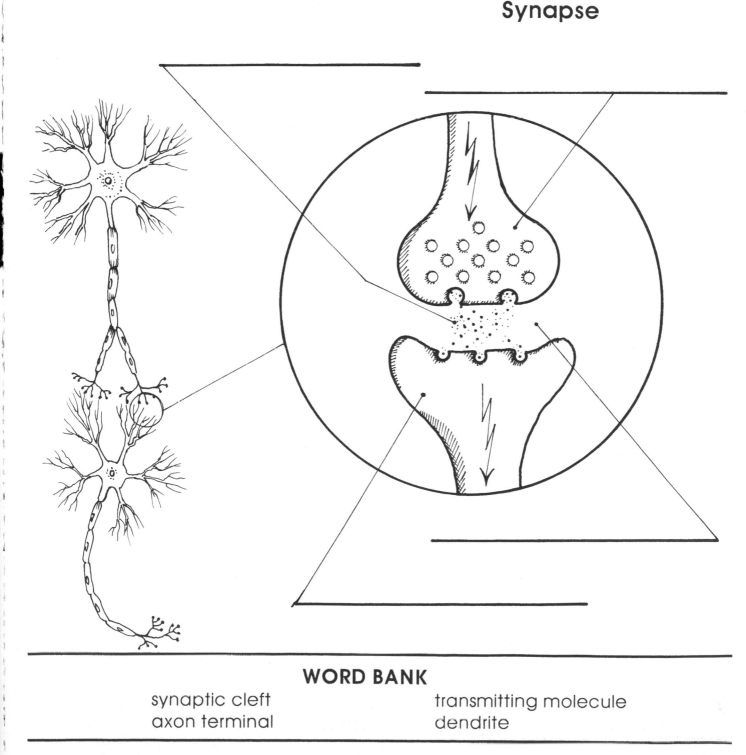

WORD BANK

synaptic cleft   transmitting molecule
axon terminal   dendrite

Exploring Your Brain

Label the parts of your brain.

Name _____

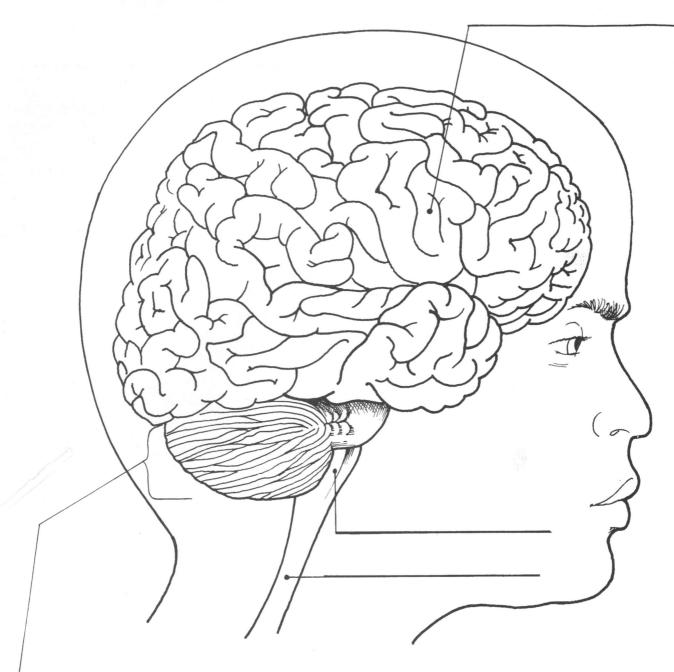

WORD BANK

cerebrum   cerebellum   brain stem
spinal cord

Nervous System

Two of the nervous systems in the human body are the **central** and the **peripheral**.

Label these two systems and their parts.

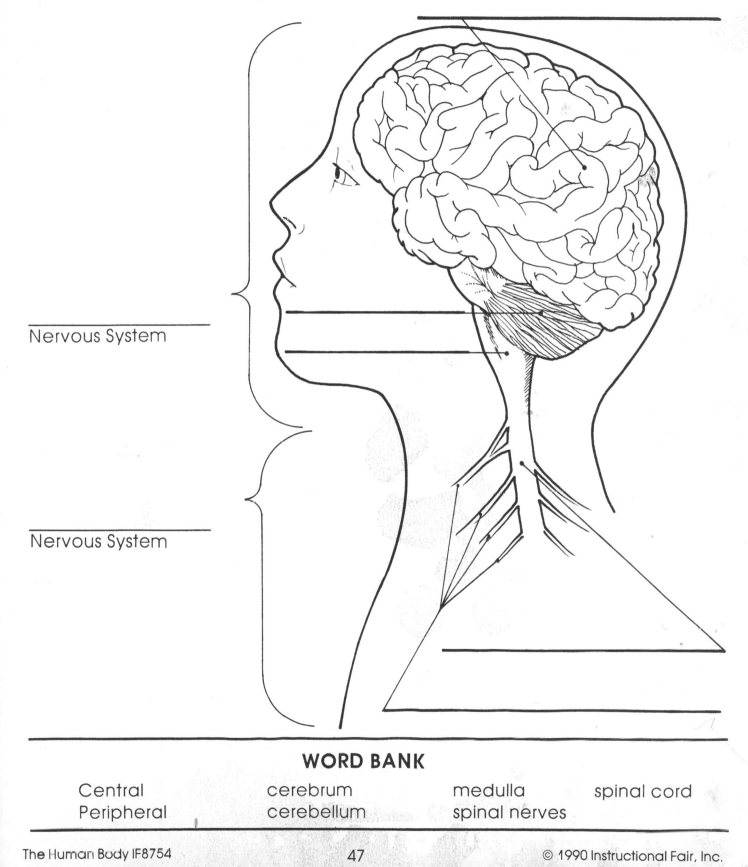

Nervous System _____

Nervous System _____

WORD BANK

Central	cerebrum	medulla	spinal cord
Peripheral	cerebellum	spinal nerves	

47

Nervous System at Work

Name _____

Write the letter of each function next to its matching part.

Draw a line from the pictured part of the nervous system to its function.

Parts

1. cerebrum _____

2. cerebellum _____

3. medulla _____

4. spinal cord _____

5. spinal nerves _____

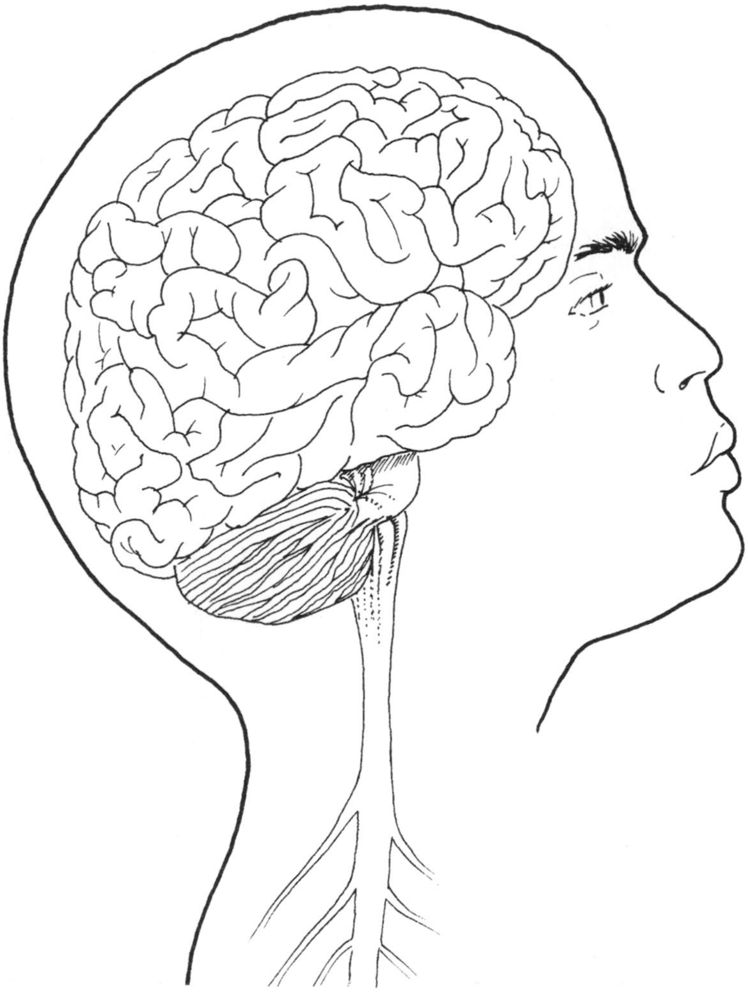

Function

a. It controls balance and muscular coordination.

b. It controls thought, voluntary movement, memory and learning, and also processes information from the senses.

c. They carry impulses between the spinal cord and body parts.

d. It controls breathing, heartbeat, and other vital body processes.

e. It relays impulses between the brain and other parts of the body.

Nervous System Functions

Label the parts of the **nervous system**.

a. _____

b. _____

c. _____

d. _____

e. _____

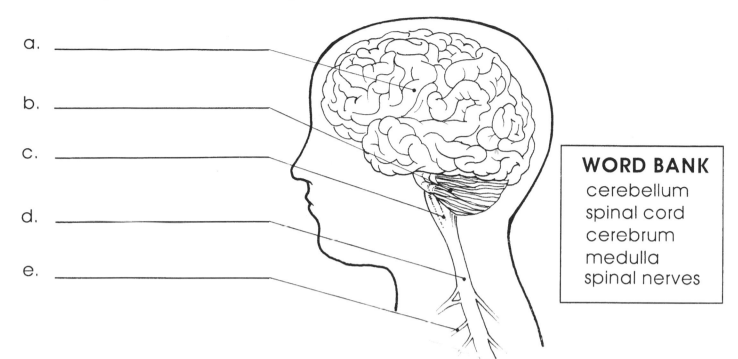

WORD BANK
cerebellum
spinal cord
cerebrum
medulla
spinal nerves

Complete the chart by writing the function of each nervous system part next to its name.

Nervous System	
Part	Function
a. _____	
b. _____	
c. _____	
d. _____	
e. _____	

Autonomic Nervous System

Name _____

The **autonomic nervous system** works almost independently of the central nervous system. It controls the life-sustaining functions of the body, such as, breathing, digestion and heartbeat. These organs and muscle tissues work involuntarily.

Label these important parts of the autonomic nervous system.

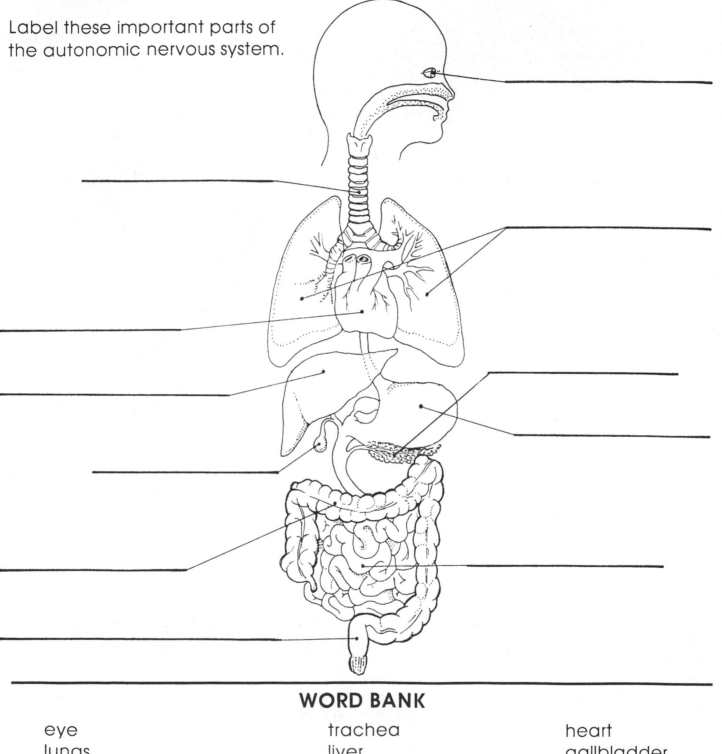

WORD BANK

eye	trachea	heart
lungs	liver	gallbladder
stomach	pancreas	small intestine
rectum	large intestine	

Control Central
(Nervous System Review)

Name _____

Use the Word Bank to complete the puzzle.

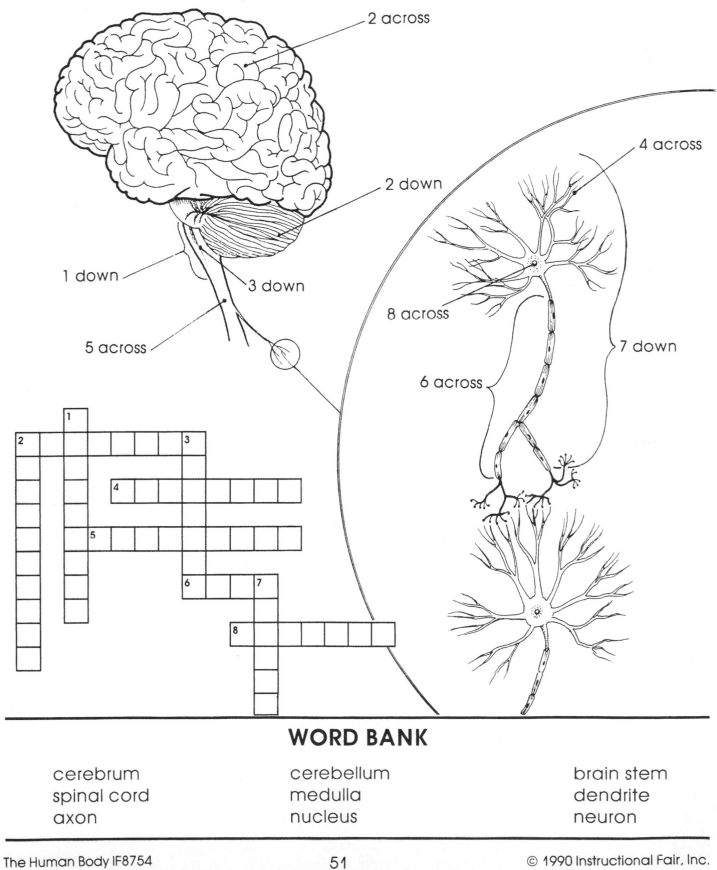

2 across

2 down

1 down

3 down

5 across

4 across

8 across

7 down

6 across

WORD BANK

cerebrum	cerebellum	brain stem
spinal cord	medulla	dendrite
axon	nucleus	neuron

Your Endocrine System

Name _____

The endocrine glands help control many of your body's functions. Using the words from the **WORD BANK**, label the glands of the Endocrine System.

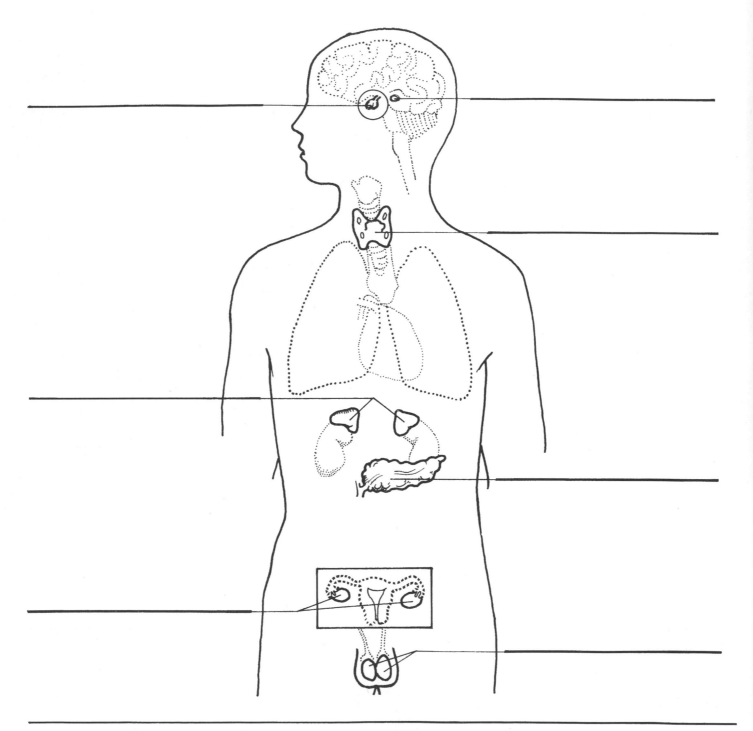

WORD BANK

thyroid gland   pituitary gland
pineal gland   pancreas
adrenal glands   ovaries (female)
testes (male)

Glands at Work

Draw a line from the name of the gland to its picture.
Draw a line from the picture of the gland to its function.

Gland   **Function**

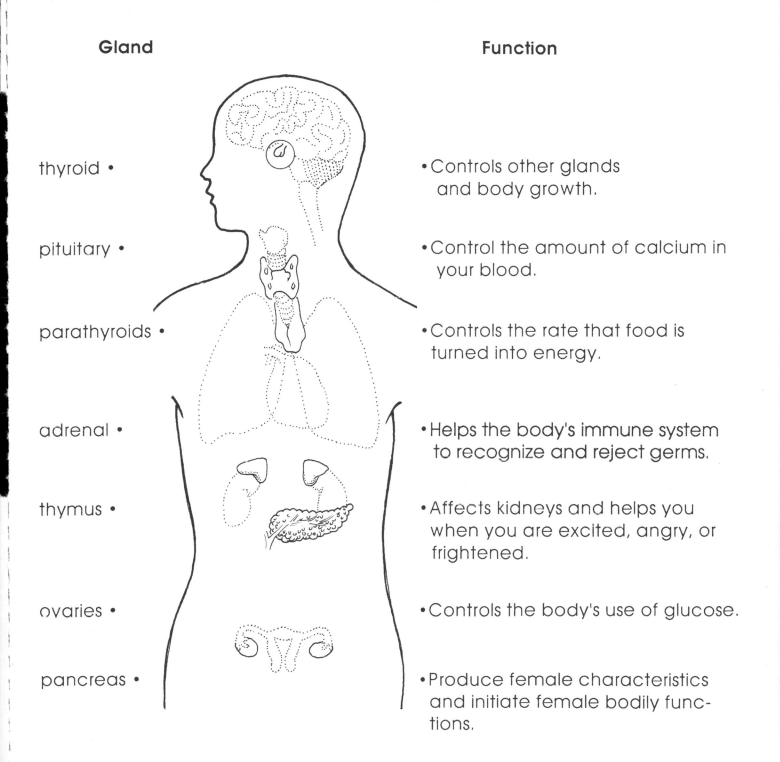

thyroid •

pituitary •

parathyroids •

adrenal •

thymus •

ovaries •

pancreas •

• Controls other glands and body growth.

• Control the amount of calcium in your blood.

• Controls the rate that food is turned into energy.

• Helps the body's immune system to recognize and reject germs.

• Affects kidneys and helps you when you are excited, angry, or frightened.

• Controls the body's use of glucose.

• Produce female characteristics and initiate female bodily functions.

Endocrine Glands

Name _____

Label each gland in the endocrine system.

a. _____

b. _____

c. _____

d. _____

e. _____

f. _____

g. _____

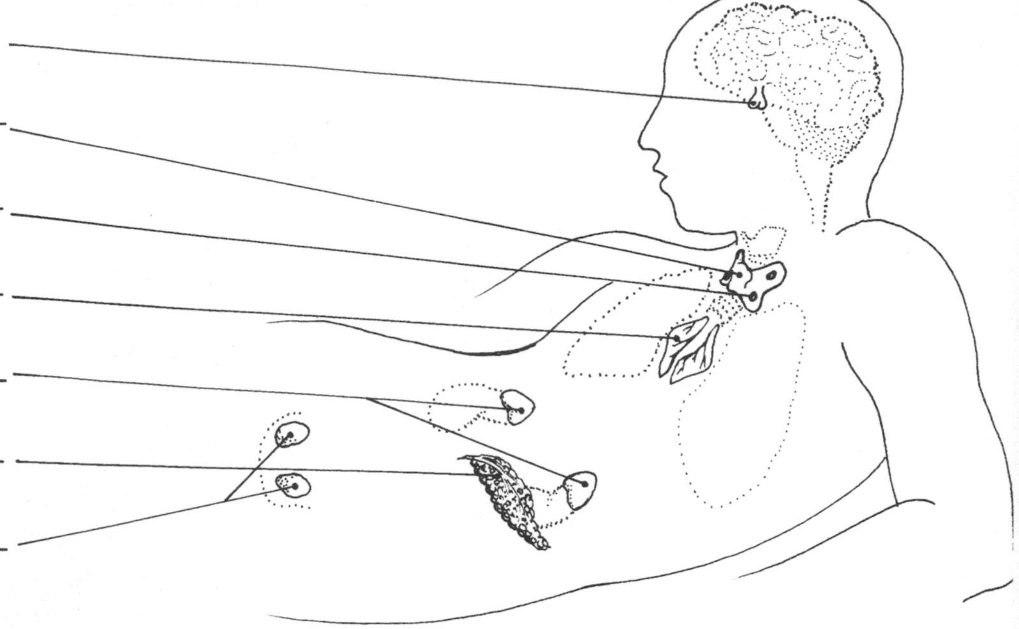

Complete the chart by writing the name of each gland and its function.

Gland	Function
a.	
b.	
c.	
d.	
e.	
f.	
g.	

WORD BANK

thyroid	parathyroids	thymus	pituitary
adrenals	pancreas	testes	

Your Sensory Systems

Name _____

Your brain gets information from outside your body through many different sense organs. Label the different sense organs and the nerve cell pictured on this page.

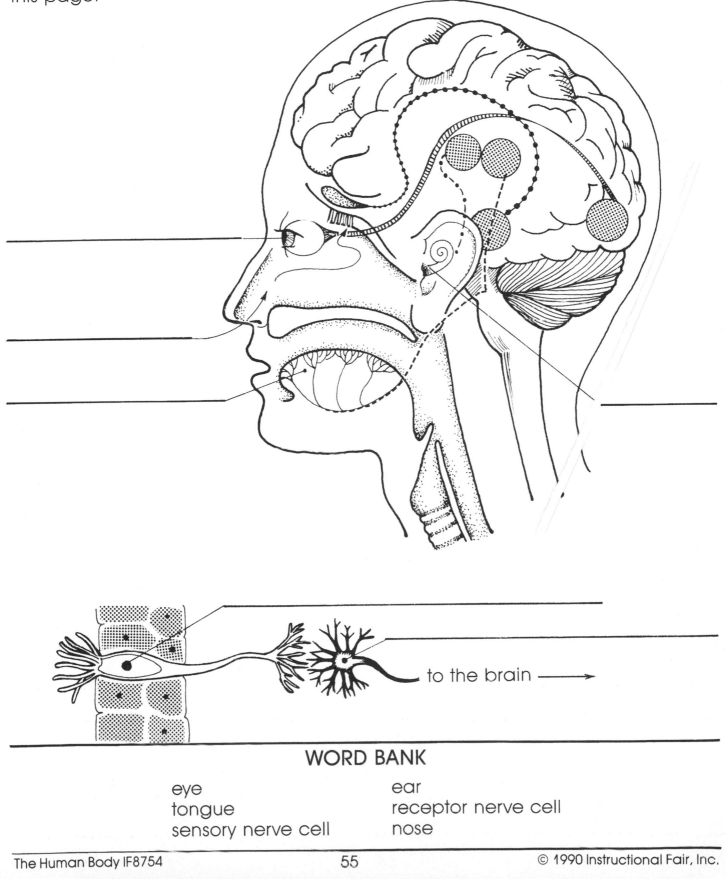

to the brain ⟶

WORD BANK

eye	ear
tongue	receptor nerve cell
sensory nerve cell	nose

It Tastes Great!

Name _____

Your tongue can sense four basic tastes—sweet, sour, bitter and salty. Label the different sense areas of the tongue and the different parts of this sense organ.

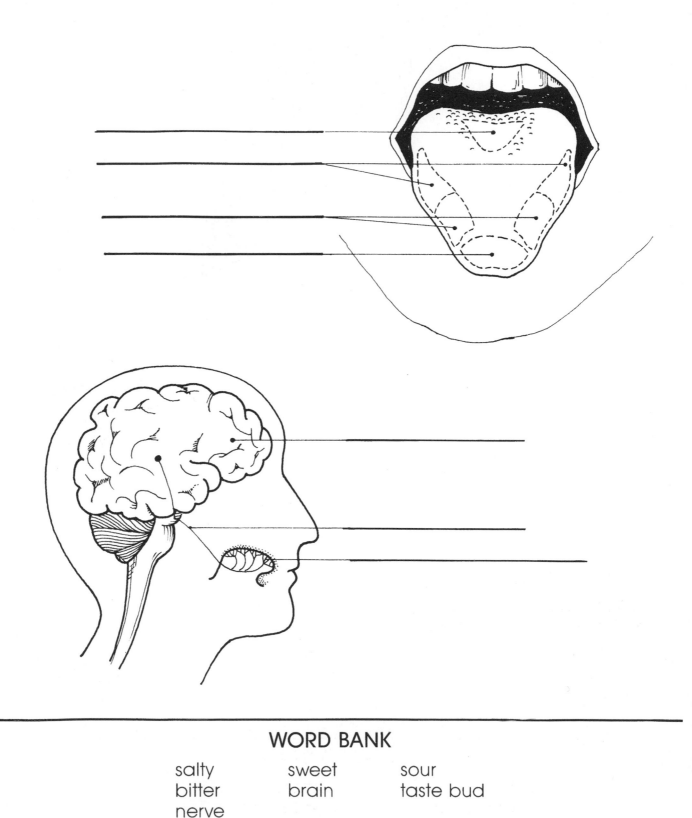

WORD BANK

salty	sweet	sour
bitter	brain	taste bud
nerve		

Your Nose

Label the parts of your nose.

Name _____

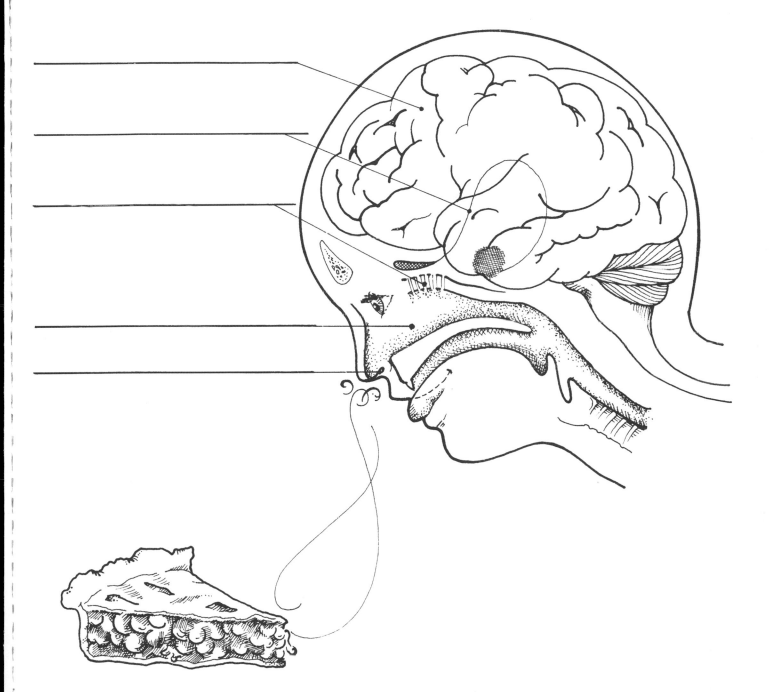

WORD BANK

nostril	olfactory nerve	brain
nasal passage	receptor cells	

Your Ear

Label the parts of your ear.

WORD BANK

auditory canal	auditory nerve	cochlea
hammer	oval window	eustachian tube
stirrup	eardrum	wax gland
semicircular canals	anvil	auricle

Your Outer Ear

Name _____

Label the three major regions of your ear, then label the parts of the outer ear.

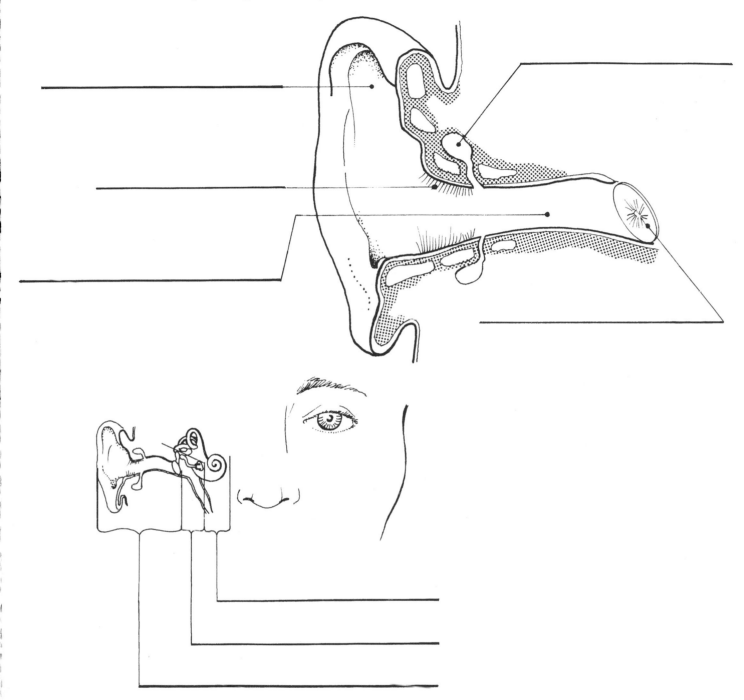

WORD BANK

outer ear	middle ear	inner ear
eardrum	auricle	auditory canal
hairs	wax gland	

Your Middle Ear

Name _____

Label the three major regions of your ear, then label the parts of the middle ear.

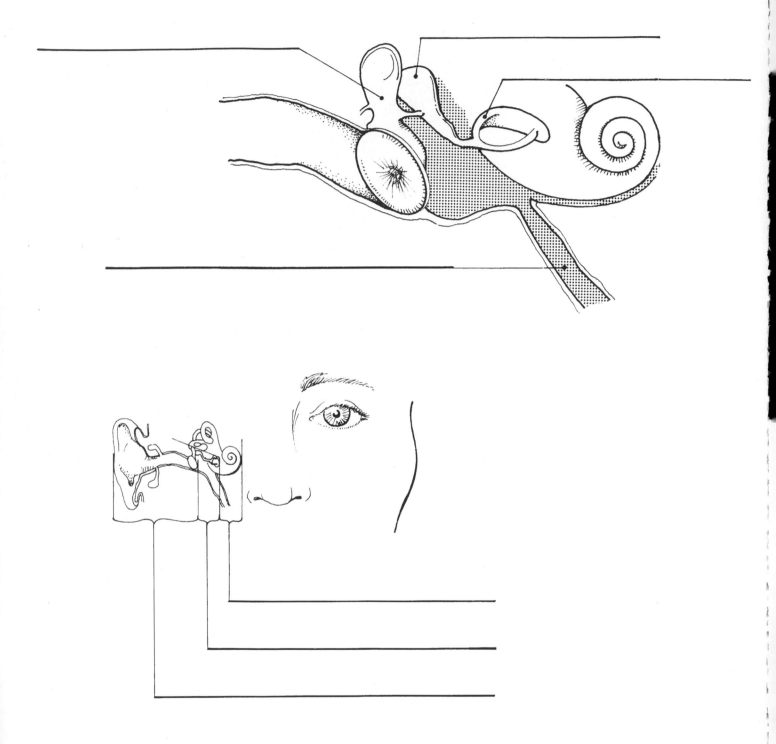

WORD BANK

middle ear   outer ear   inner ear
hammer   anvil   stirrup
eustachian tube

Your Inner Ear

Name _____

Label the three major regions of your ear, then label the parts of the inner ear.

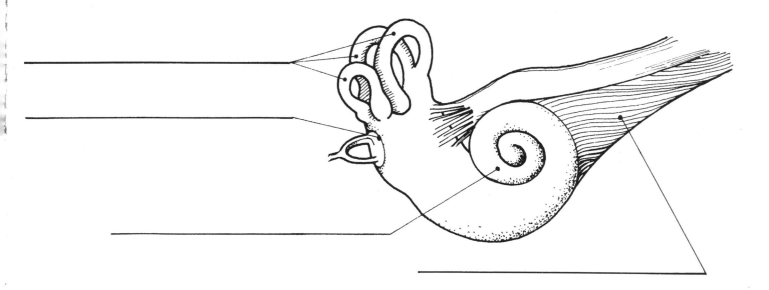

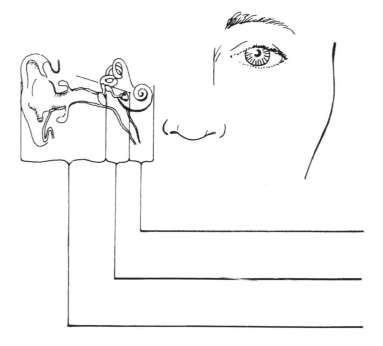

WORD BANK

inner ear   outer ear   middle ear

cochlea   auditory nerve

oval window   semicircular canals

Ear, Nose and Throat Connection

Name _____

Your ears, nose, mouth and throat are all connected to each other. Label the parts in the picture below.

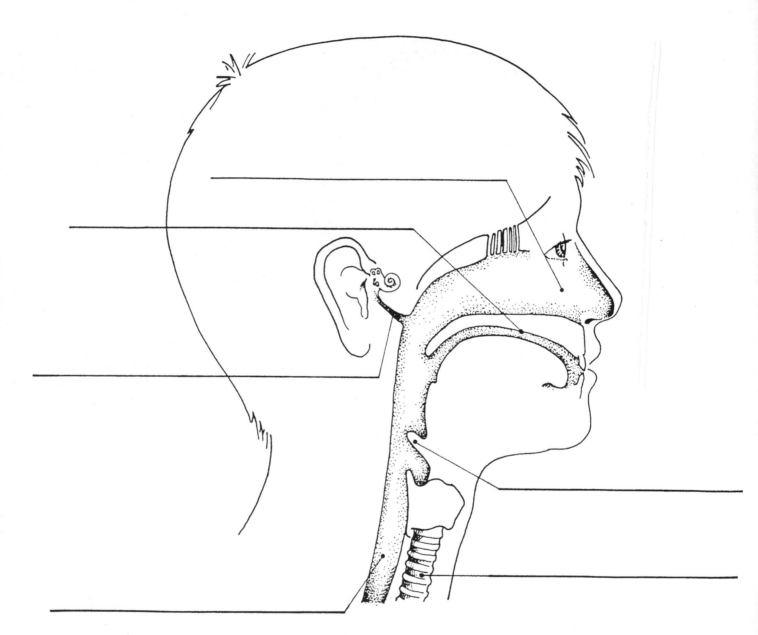

WORD BANK

windpipe   food tube   nasal passage
epiglottis   eustachian tube   roof of the mouth

Your Eye

Name _____

Label the parts of your eye pictured below.

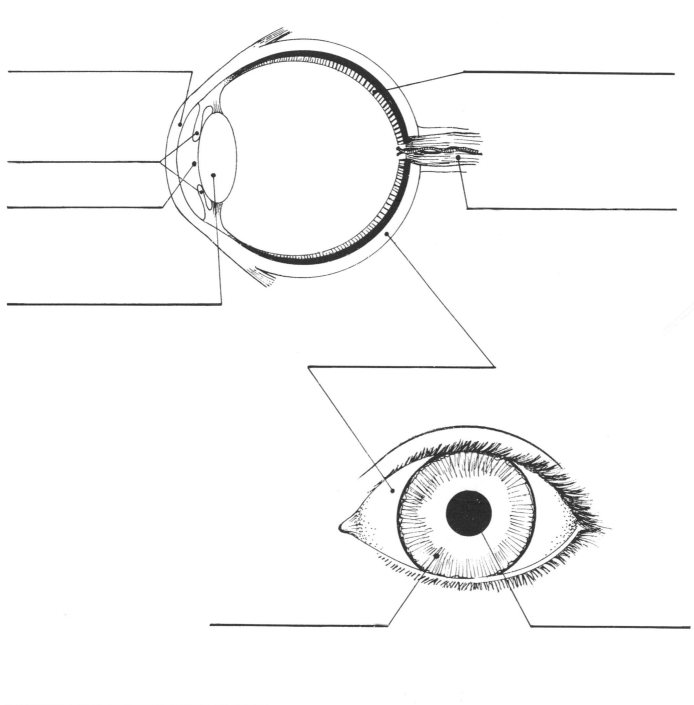

WORD BANK

optic nerve   retina   lens
iris   cornea   pupil
sclera

Inside Your Eye

Label the parts of your eye pictured below.

Name _____

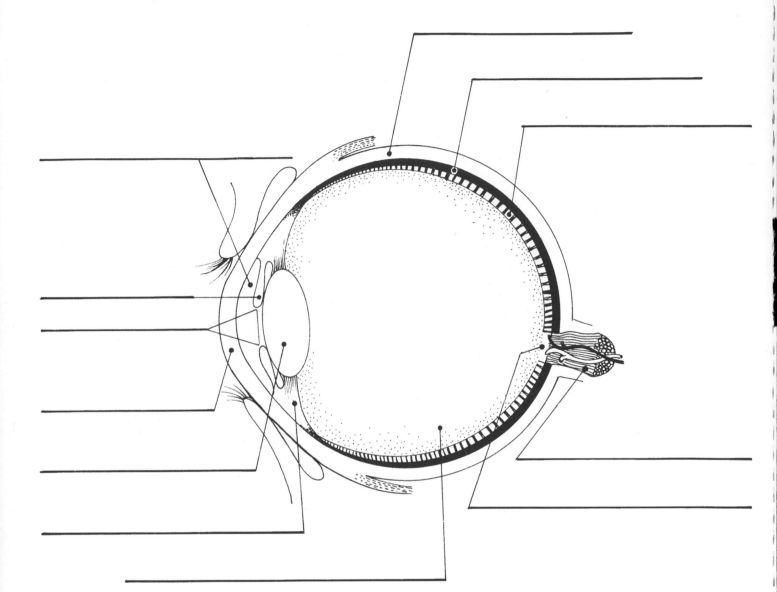

WORD BANK

optic nerve	retina	vitreous humor (clear jelly)
lens	iris	ciliary muscles (lens controlling muscles)
cornea	pupil	sclera
blind spot	choroid	aqueous humor (watery fluid)

Eyes to Brain Connection

Name _____

Your eyes gather the rays of light coming off an object. They change the light rays into nerve impulses, but your brain interprets these impulses and "draws" a picture of the image. Label the parts of this "Eye to Brain Connection".

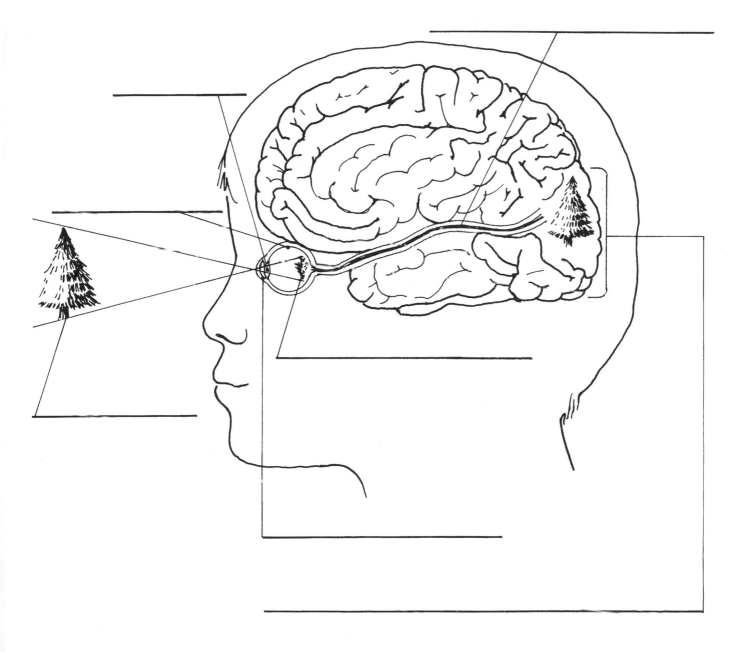

WORD BANK

image	cornea	lens
retina	optic nerve	visual cortex
upside-down image		

Eye Protection

Name _____

Your eyeball is very well protected. Label the parts of the eye and those that help protect it.

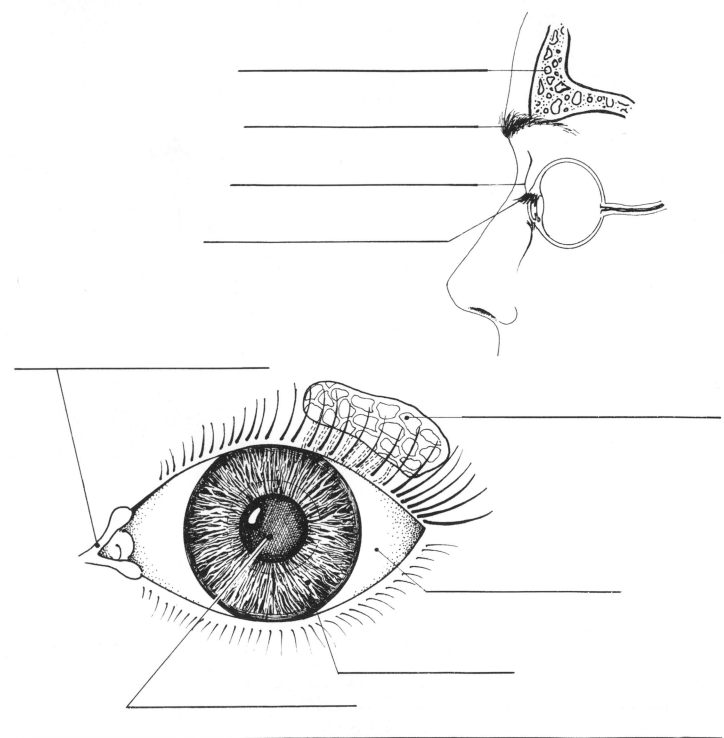

WORD BANK

pupil	iris	sclera
eyelid	eyelash	tear gland
tear duct	skull	eyebrow

Your Eye—The Camera

Name _____

Your eye is very similar to a camera. Label the parts of the eye and the camera. Also, give the job of each part.

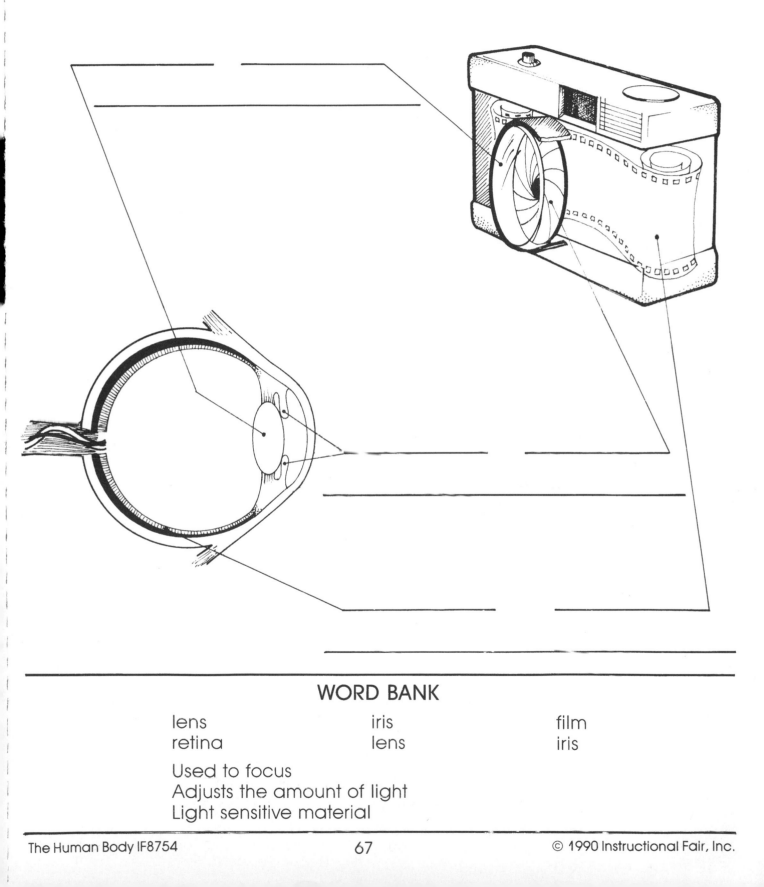

WORD BANK

lens	iris	film
retina	lens	iris

Used to focus
Adjusts the amount of light
Light sensitive material

Your Eyesight

Name _____

Eyes can vary in shape. This can give people problems with their sight. Using the words from the **WORD BANK**, label the eyes below.

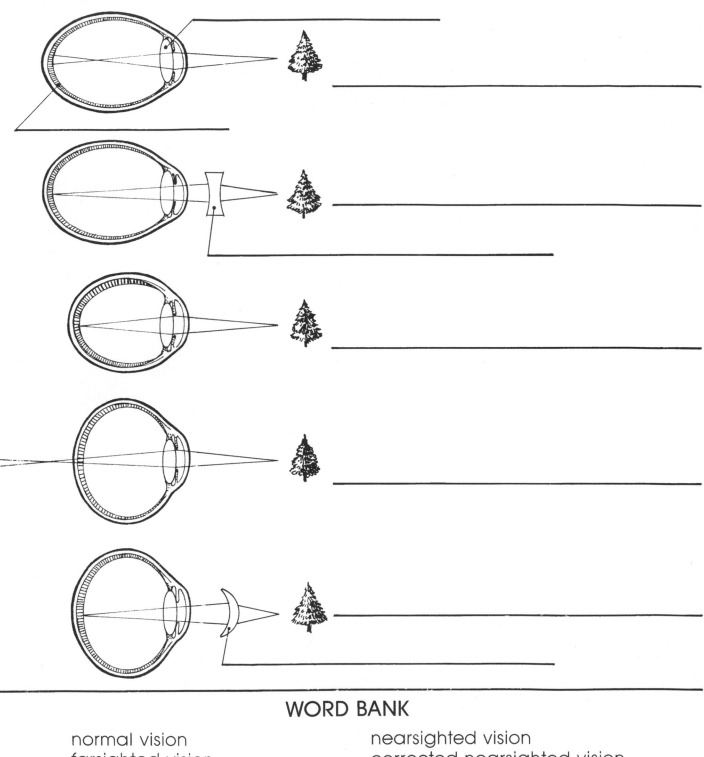

_____

_____

_____

_____

_____

_____

WORD BANK

normal vision
farsighted vision
corrected farsighted vision
concave lens
lens

nearsighted vision
corrected nearsighted vision
convex lens
retina

Sensational!
(Ear and Eye Review)

Name _____

Use the Word Bank to complete the puzzle.

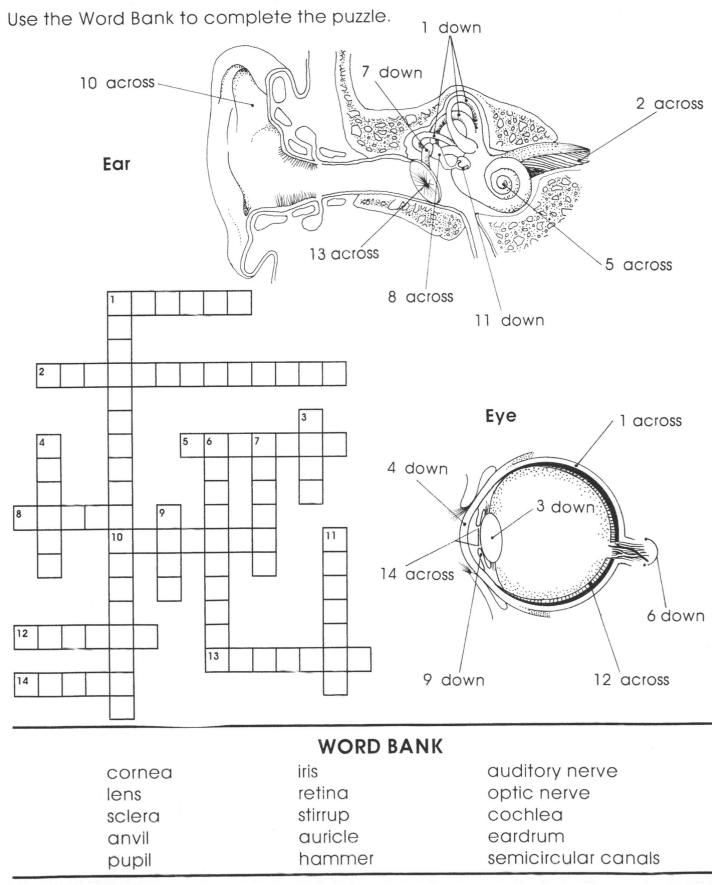

Ear

10 across
1 down
7 down
2 across
13 across
5 across
8 across
11 down

Eye

1 across
4 down
3 down
14 across
6 down
9 down
12 across

WORD BANK

cornea	iris	auditory nerve
lens	retina	optic nerve
sclera	stirrup	cochlea
anvil	auricle	eardrum
pupil	hammer	semicircular canals

Skin Deep

Your skin is made up of many layers. These layers contain hairs, nerves, blood vessels and glands. Label these layers and other parts using the words from the **WORD BANK**.

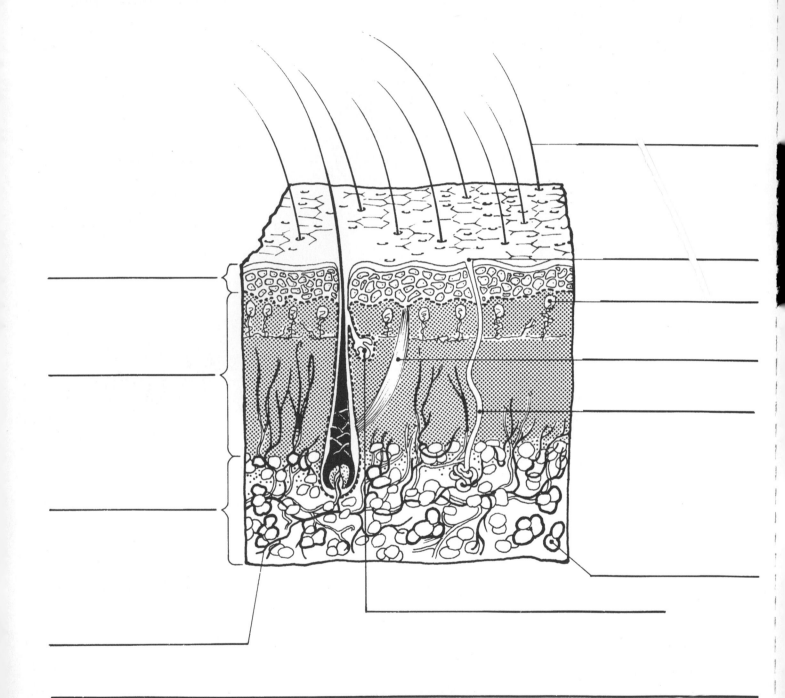

WORD BANK

epidermis	dermis	fat layer	hair muscle
fat cells	hair	oil gland	blood vessel
sweat gland	pore	nerve	

How a Pimple Develops

Name _____

Pimples begin to form when sebum, an oily substance given off by the sebaceous gland, gets trapped beneath the surface of the skin.

Number the three stages pictured below. Label the parts illustrated in each stage.

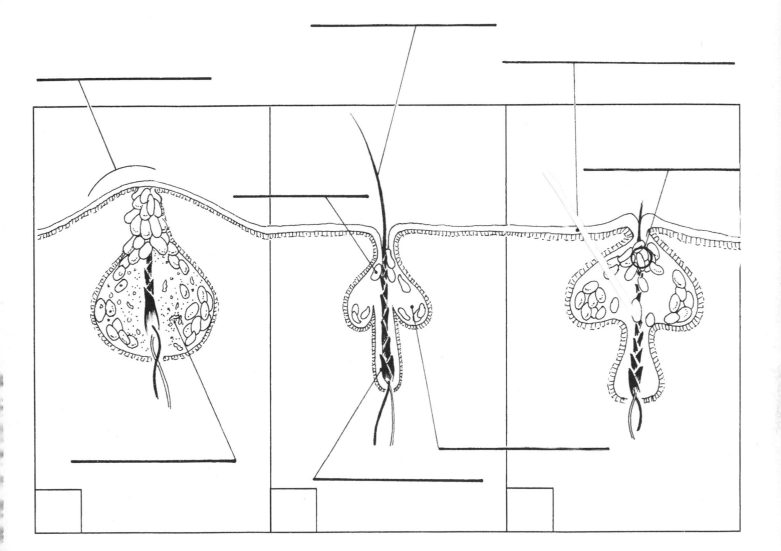

WORD BANK

hair follicle	hair	pus	pimple
sebaceous gland	sebum	blockage	epidermis

Sweaty Palms and Goose Bumps

Name _____

Your body has its own air conditioning system. On cold days your skin has a way to keep in your body's warmth. On hot days your skin can cool you off.

Label the two pictures either **WARM DAY** or **COOL DAY**. Label the parts of the skin using the words from the **WORD BANK**.

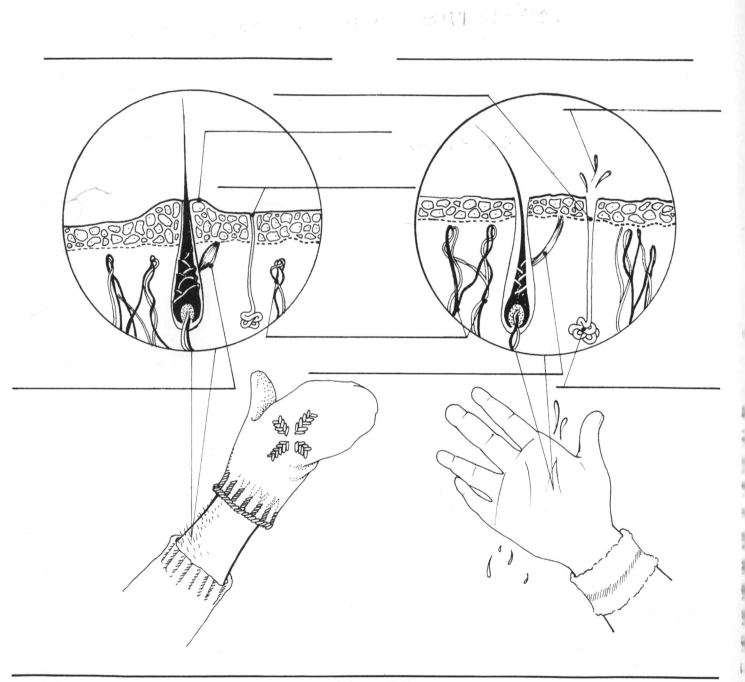

WORD BANK

closed sweat pore	open sweat pore
relaxed muscle	contracted muscle
sweat gland	blood vessels
goose bump	sweat

Body Tissues

Name _____

Many of the body's organs are made of a variety of tissues working together. There are four kinds of tissue: **connective, epithelial, muscle, and nerve.** Each has a specialized function.

Study the pictures and read the descriptions. Write the name of each tissue beneath its description. Then label the tissue parts in each picture.

Composed of relatively few cells and surrounded by larger amounts of nonliving material. Supports and connects other tissues.

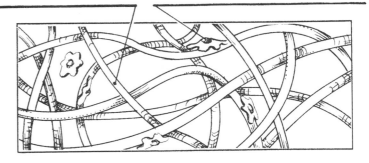

_____

Made up of cells that can contract and relax. Allows the body to make internal and external movements.

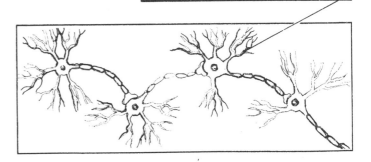

_____

Specialized cells which carry electrical signals between the brain and other parts of the body.

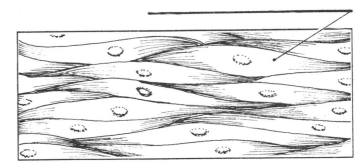

_____

Tightly-packed cells which form a covering for the skin and line the hollow internal organs.

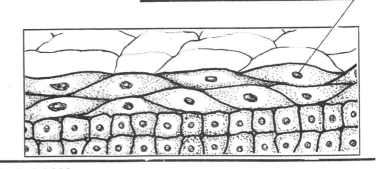

_____

WORD BANK

connective tissue	epithelial tissue	muscle tissue
nerve tissue	collagen	fibroblast
nerve fiber	cell nucleus	cell

Fingerprints

The ridges in fingertips form unique patterns. No two people have the same pattern, not even identical twins. The ridges on fingers form three main groups of patterns – the arch, the loop, and the whorl.

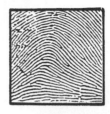

arch

loop

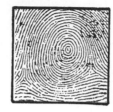

whorl

Make a record of your own fingerprints on the chart below by . . .

a. placing the side of your fingertip on an inkpad and rolling your finger from one side to the other.

b. then placing the side of each inked finger on the chart and rolling it softly to leave a clear, crisp print.

c. labeling each print using the examples at the top of this page as a guide.

Right Hand

Thumb	Index	Middle	Ring	Little

Left Hand

Little	Ring	Middle	Index	Thumb

Your Toenails and Fingernails

Name _____

Nails are a specialized part of your skin that protect the ends of your toes and fingers. Label the parts of the nails below.

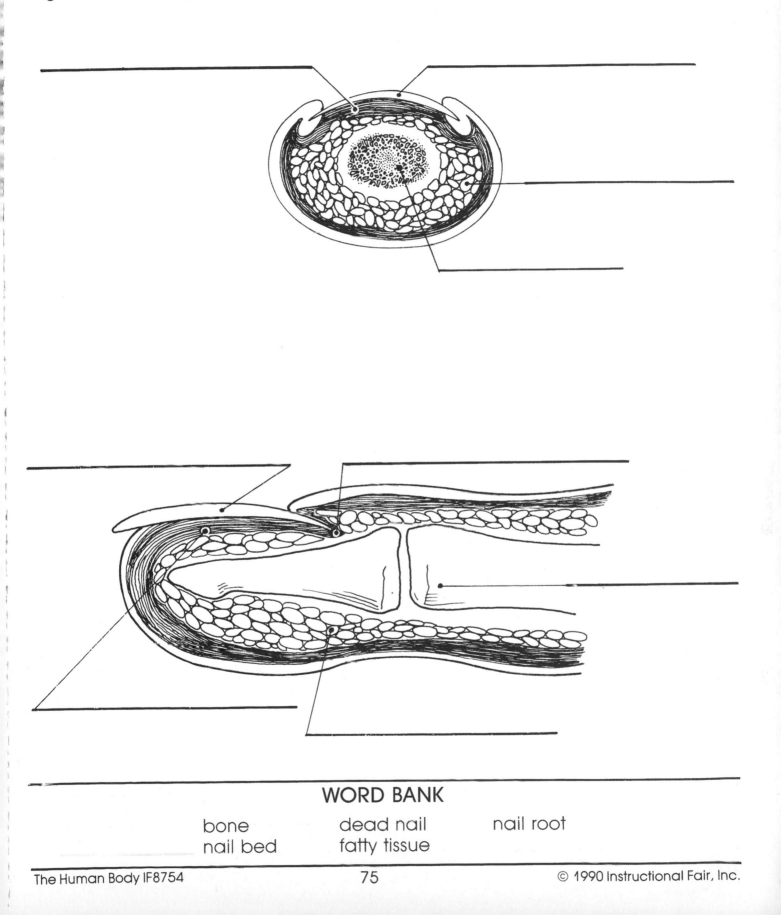

WORD BANK

bone	dead nail	nail root
nail bed	fatty tissue	

Reproductive System—Male

Name _____

The purpose of the Reproductive System is to create new life. Label the parts of the Male Reproductive System.

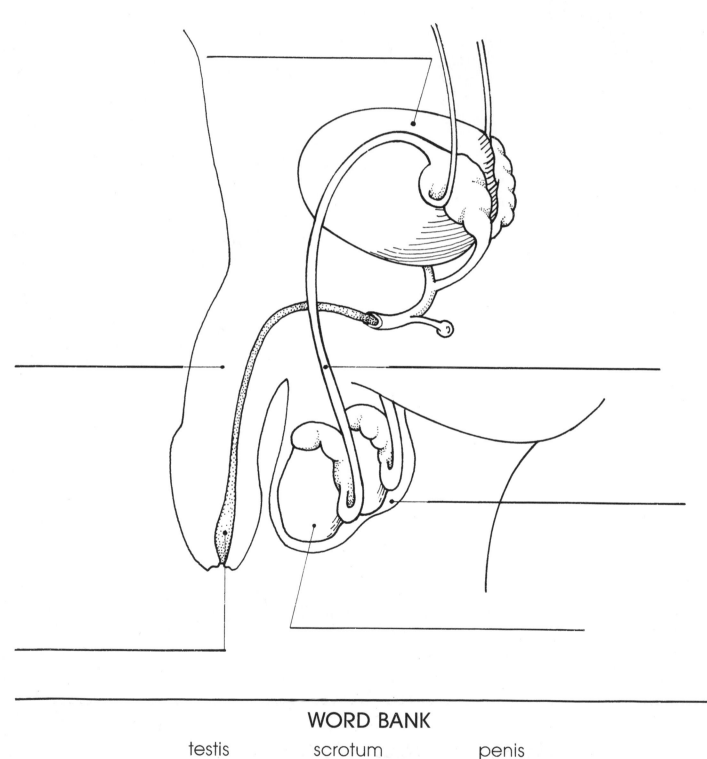

WORD BANK

testis	scrotum	penis
urethra	sperm tube	bladder

Reproductive System—Female

Name _____

The purpose of the Reproductive System is to create new life. Label the parts of the Female Reproductive System.

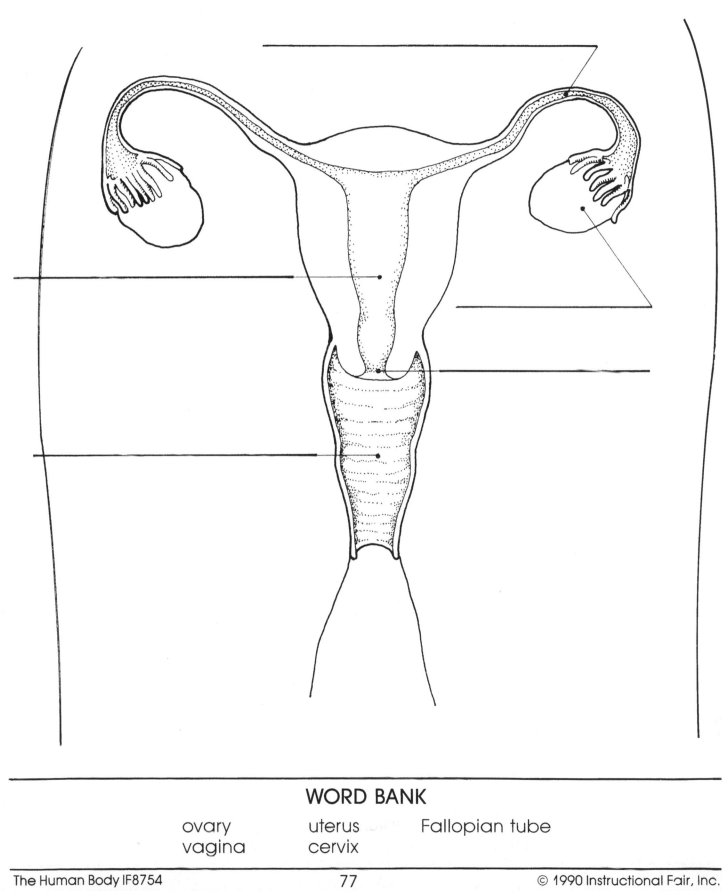

WORD BANK

ovary	uterus	Fallopian tube
vagina	cervix	

New Life

Name _____

From the time of conception, a single cell divides and keeps on dividing until it forms the six trillion cells of a human newborn baby. This development takes nine months.

Beneath each picture write the matching description from the Word Bank of a baby's development.

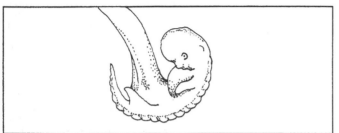

4 weeks

_____

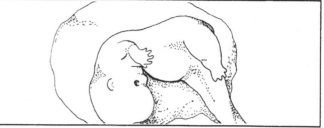

8 weeks

_____

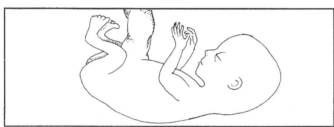

3 months

_____

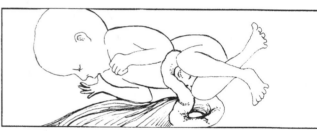

4-6 months

_____

7 months

_____

_____

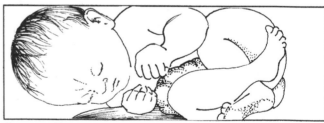

9 months

_____

_____

WORD BANK

Fully developed with organs that can function on their own.
Develops tiny arm and leg buds, and its heart begins to beat.
Ears, eyes, nose, fingers, and toes are formed.
Can survive birth with special care.
First movements felt and heartbeat can be heard with a stethoscope.
Has recognizable human features and sex can be determined.

Birth of a Baby

Name _____

When a baby is fully developed within the uterus, a hormone in the pituitary gland stimulates the muscles of the uterus. These muscle contractions signal the beginning of labor. The opening to the uterus, the cervix, gradually enlarges to allow the baby to pass through. The amniotic sac that surrounds the baby will break, releasing a gush of amniotic fluid. After the baby is born the placenta separates from the wall of the uterus and is pushed out by more muscle contractions.

Study and label the diagram of the birth of a baby.

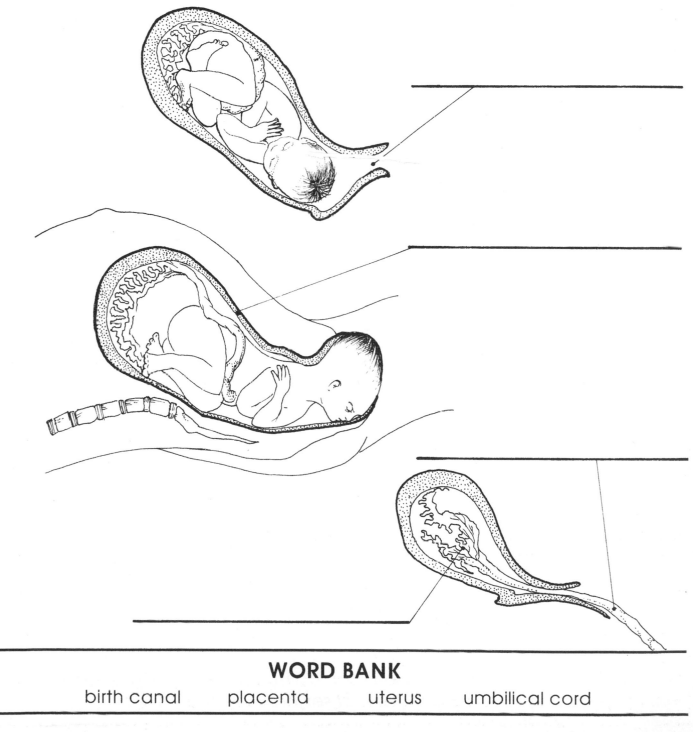

WORD BANK

birth canal   placenta   uterus   umbilical cord

Designer "Genes"

Name _____

There are more than 40,000 **genes** that determine traits each person has. These traits such as, dark hair, blue eyes, etc., are inherited from parents. There are two strengths of traits: **dominant** - being the strongest, and **recessive** - the weakest.

Place checks in each chart to show who would have the dominant and/or recessive genes in each category.

D = Dominant Trait   R = Recessive Trait

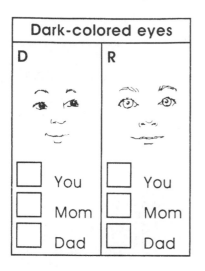

Dark-colored eyes

D	R
☐ You	☐ You
☐ Mom	☐ Mom
☐ Dad	☐ Dad

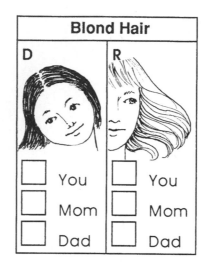

Blond Hair

D	R
☐ You	☐ You
☐ Mom	☐ Mom
☐ Dad	☐ Dad

Dimples

D	R
☐ You	☐ You
☐ Mom	☐ Mom
☐ Dad	☐ Dad

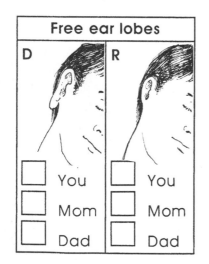

Free ear lobes

D	R
☐ You	☐ You
☐ Mom	☐ Mom
☐ Dad	☐ Dad

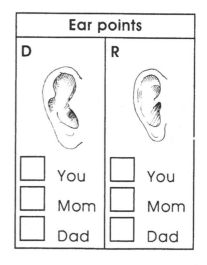

Ear points

D	R
☐ You	☐ You
☐ Mom	☐ Mom
☐ Dad	☐ Dad

Designer "Genes"
(cont'd.)

Name _____

D = Dominant Trait   R = Recessive Trait

Can roll tongue	
D	**R**

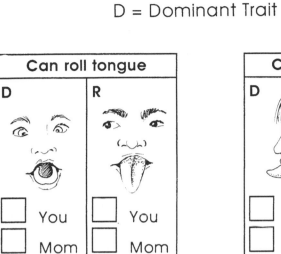

D	R
☐ You	☐ You
☐ Mom	☐ Mom
☐ Dad	☐ Dad

Can fold tongue	
D	**R**

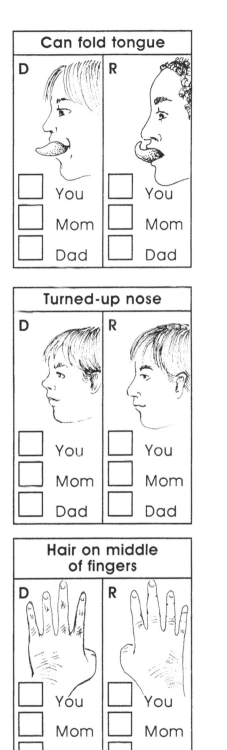

D	R
☐ You	☐ You
☐ Mom	☐ Mom
☐ Dad	☐ Dad

Clockwise hair whorl	
D	**R**

D	R
☐ You	☐ You
☐ Mom	☐ Mom
☐ Dad	☐ Dad

Widow's peak
D   **R**

D	R
☐ You	☐ You
☐ Mom	☐ Mom
☐ Dad	☐ Dad

Turned-up nose
D   **R**

D	R
☐ You	☐ You
☐ Mom	☐ Mom
☐ Dad	☐ Dad

Dark hair
D   **R**

D	R
☐ You	☐ You
☐ Mom	☐ Mom
☐ Dad	☐ Dad

Freckles
D   **R**

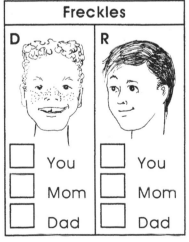

D	R
☐ You	☐ You
☐ Mom	☐ Mom
☐ Dad	☐ Dad

Hair on middle of fingers
D   **R**

D	R
☐ You	☐ You
☐ Mom	☐ Mom
☐ Dad	☐ Dad

Bent little finger
D   **R**

D	R
☐ You	☐ You
☐ Mom	☐ Mom
☐ Dad	☐ Dad

Name _____

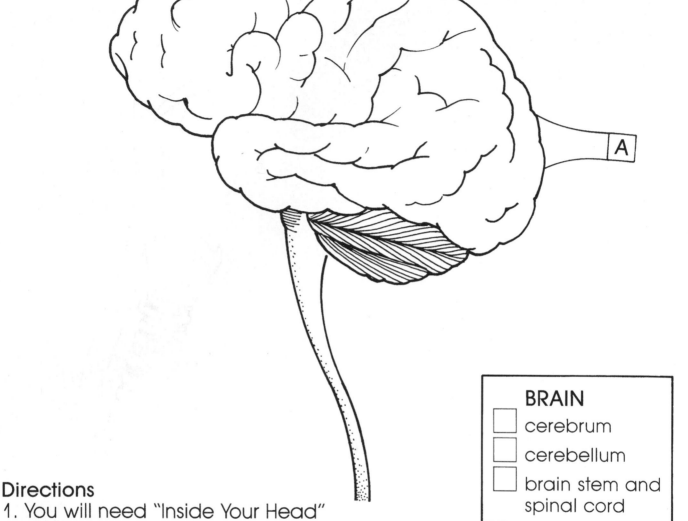

A

BRAIN
- [ ] cerebrum
- [ ] cerebellum
- [ ] brain stem and spinal cord

Directions

1. You will need "Inside Your Head" pages A, B, C and D.

2. Color the keys on pages A, B and C. Then, use the keys to color the head parts.

3. Cut out the head parts and keys on pages A, B and C.

4. Glue the tabs of the head parts and the keys onto the head outline on page D.

5. Overlap the different head parts on the head outline. Notice the locations of the various head parts.

Inside Your Head (Page B)

Name _____

BREATHING

- ☐ nasal passage
- ☐ windpipe
- ☐ voice box
- ☐ esophagus
- ☐ tongue
- ☐ epiglottis
- ☐ palate

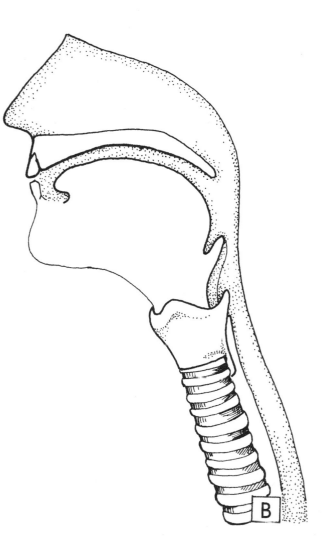

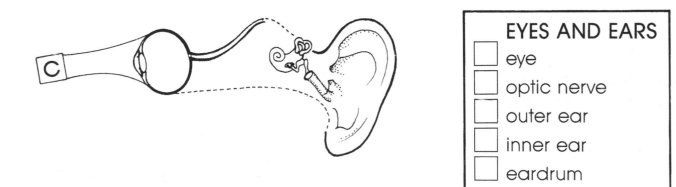

EYES AND EARS

- ☐ eye
- ☐ optic nerve
- ☐ outer ear
- ☐ inner ear
- ☐ eardrum

Name _____

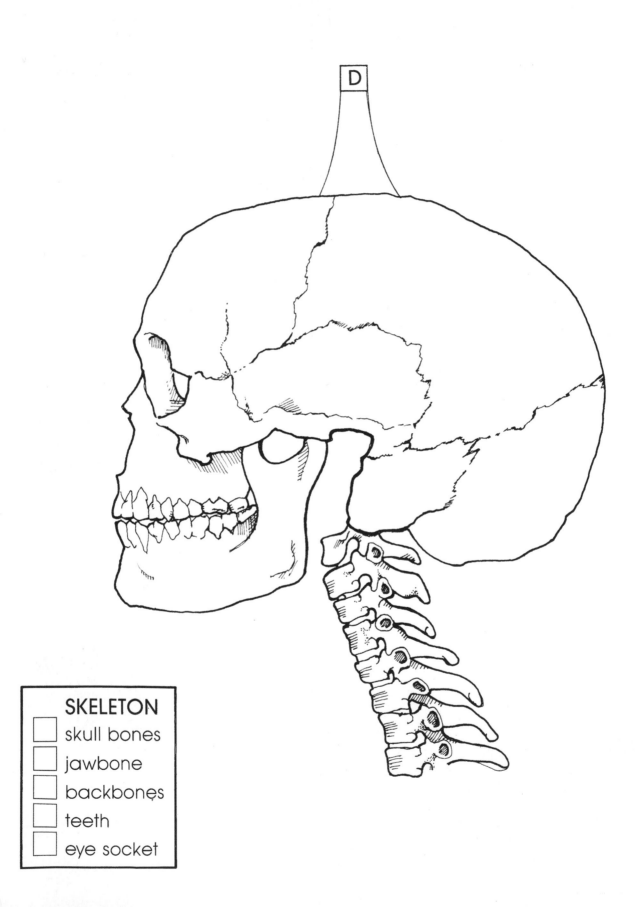

SKELETON
- [ ] skull bones
- [ ] jawbone
- [ ] backbones
- [ ] teeth
- [ ] eye socket

Inside Your Head (Page D)

Name _____

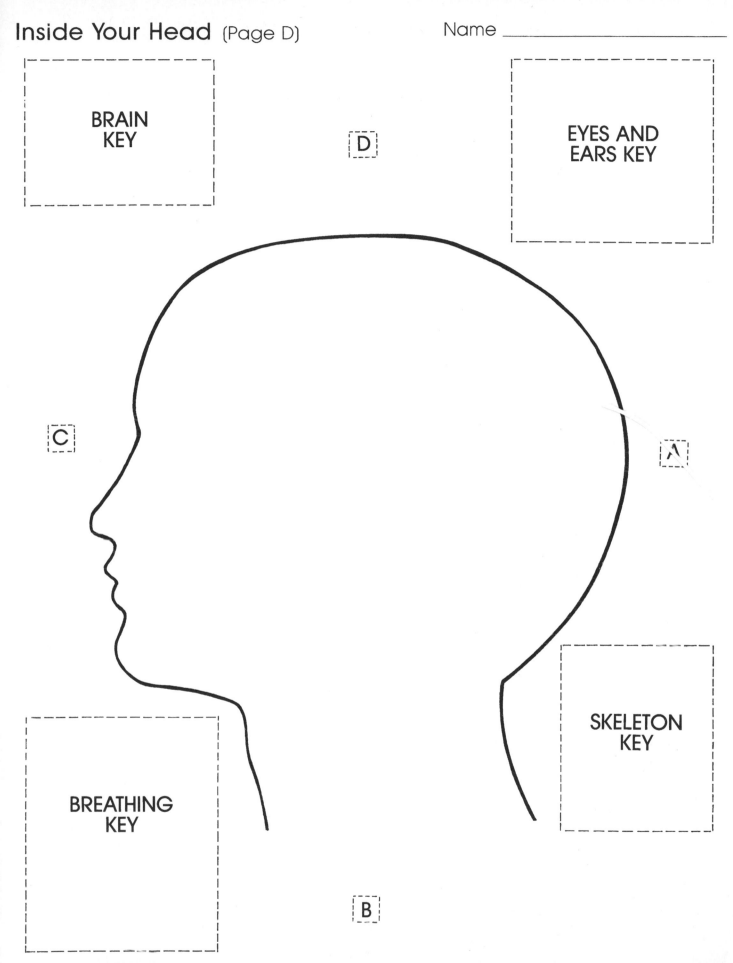

BRAIN
KEY

D

EYES AND
EARS KEY

C

A

SKELETON
KEY

BREATHING
KEY

B

Your Visible Body (Page A)

Name _____

Glue pages **A** and **B** by overlapping the stars of page **A** over the stars of page **B**.

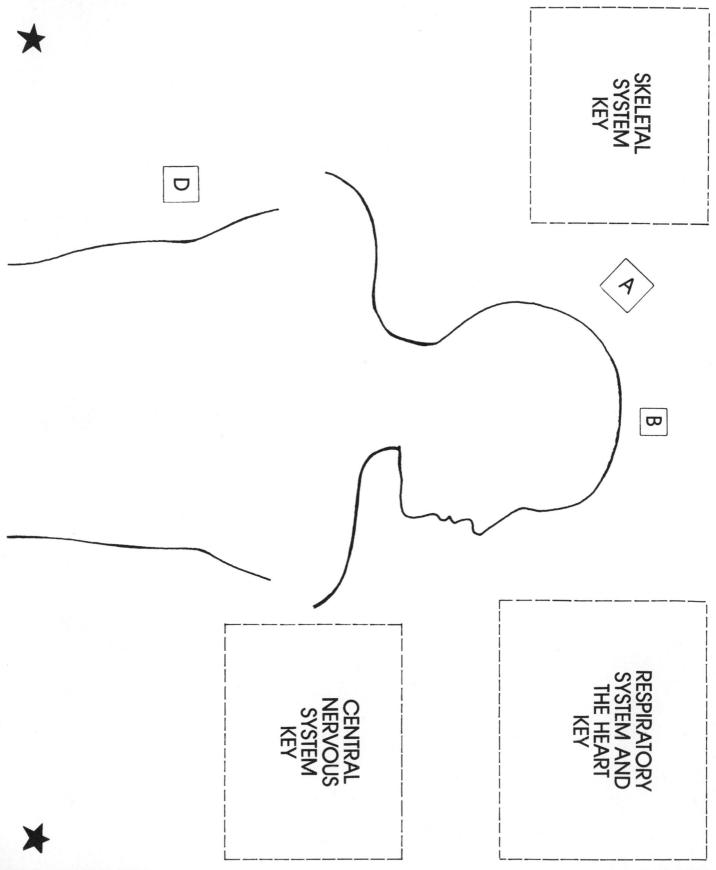

SKELETAL
SYSTEM
KEY

D

A

B

RESPIRATORY
SYSTEM AND
THE HEART
KEY

CENTRAL
NERVOUS
SYSTEM
KEY

Name _____

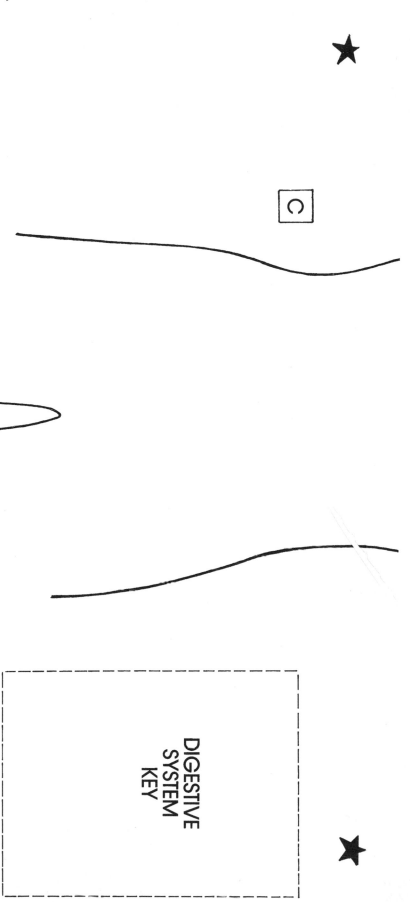

DIGESTIVE
SYSTEM
KEY

Your Visible Body (Page C)

Name _____

On pages **C**, **D** and **E** are pictures of four body systems. Next to each body system is a "key" that lists the parts of the system.

1. Color each of the body parts of a body system a different color.

2. Color the boxes in the key to match the parts of the system.

3. Cut out the body systems and keys on pages **C**, **D** and **E**.

4. Glue the tabs of each body system on the spaces that are marked on pages **A** and **B**.

5. Glue the keys in the spaces that are marked on pages **A** and **B**.

You are now ready to overlap the different body systems. This will show you where each system is located in your body.

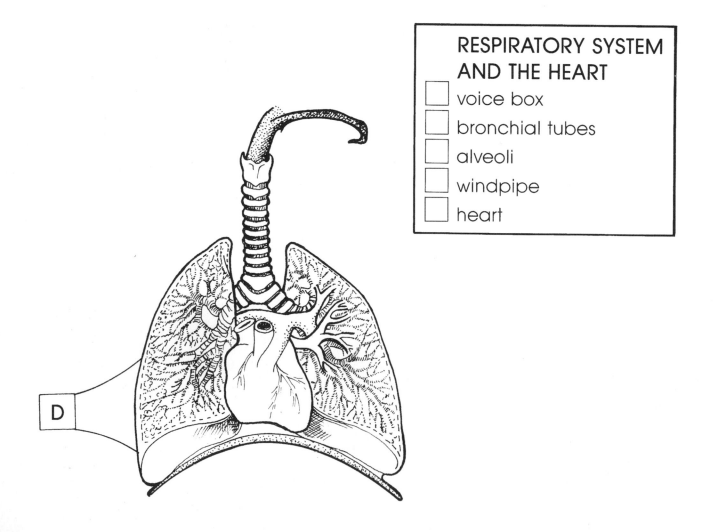

RESPIRATORY SYSTEM AND THE HEART
- ☐ voice box
- ☐ bronchial tubes
- ☐ alveoli
- ☐ windpipe
- ☐ heart

Your Visible Body (Page D)

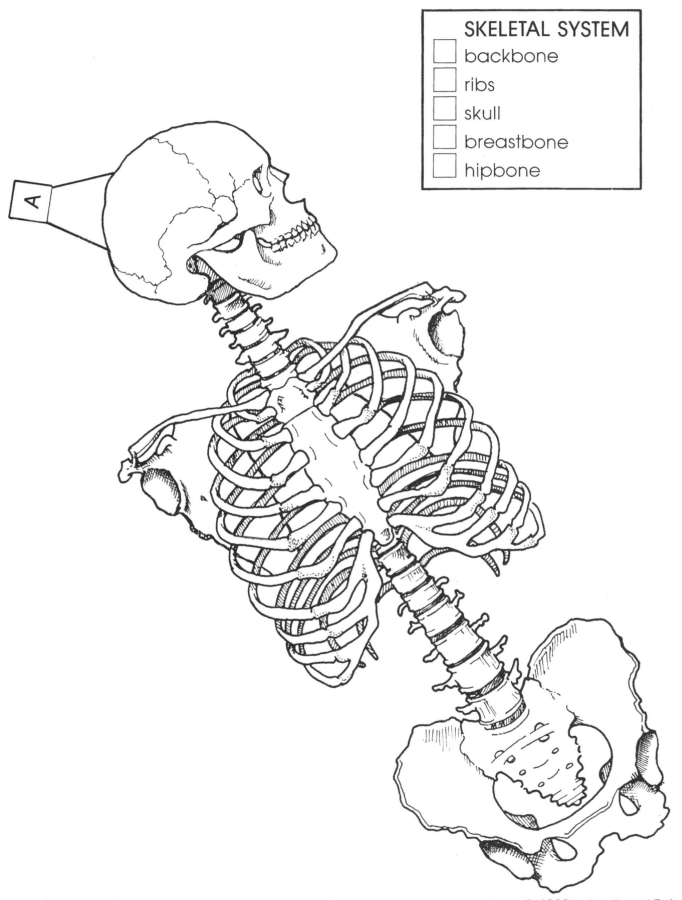

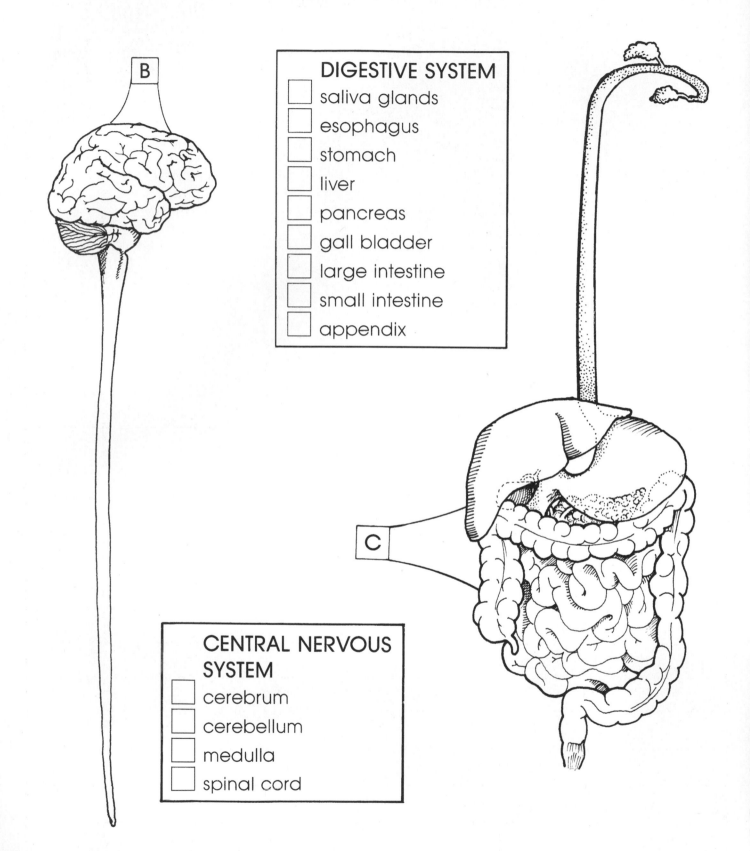

B

DIGESTIVE SYSTEM
- [ ] saliva glands
- [ ] esophagus
- [ ] stomach
- [ ] liver
- [ ] pancreas
- [ ] gall bladder
- [ ] large intestine
- [ ] small intestine
- [ ] appendix

C

CENTRAL NERVOUS SYSTEM
- [ ] cerebrum
- [ ] cerebellum
- [ ] medulla
- [ ] spinal cord

Organg Systems

Name _____

Make an "X" in the correct box to show to which system/systems each organ belongs. One is done for you.

Organs	Systems						
	Diges-tive	Respi-ratory	Urinary	Repro-ductive	Circu-latory	Nervous	Endo-crine
Bladder			X				
Brain							
Heart							
Ovaries							
Liver							
Pancreas							
Kidneys							
Spinal Cord							
Lungs							
Small Intestines							
Diaphragm							
Mouth							
Nerves							
Testes							
Thyroid Gland							
Arteries							
Esophagus							
Cerebellum							

Think Fast!

Name _____

The time it takes for your ears to send a message to your brain, and your body to respond is called **reaction time.**

Let's try an experiment to test your reaction time.

Materials: 30 cm metric ruler.

Procedure:

1. Place your left arm on a table with your hand over the edge.

2. Space your thumb and index fingers about 4 cm apart.

3. Have a partner hold the "30 cm end" of the ruler, with the other end just above your open thumb and index finger.

4. Your partner will say "set," and drop the ruler.

5. Catch the ruler with your thumb and index finger as quickly as possible.

6. Check the distance fallen by taking a reading at the bottom of the index finger.

7. Record your results.

8. Repeat the procedure 10 times with each hand.

Are you right-handed, or left-handed? Which of your hands was the quickest?

_____

Did others find the same results?

_____

Trial #	Reaction Distance	
	Left Hand	Right Hand
1.		
2.		
3.		
4.		
5.		
6.		
7.		
8.		
9.		
10.		

Feel the Beat

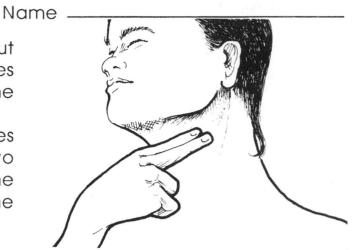

When the heart pumps, it forces blood out into the arteries. The walls of the arteries expand and contract to the rhythm of the heart which creates a **pulse.**

You can feel your pulse where the arteries are close to the surface of the skin. Two good places to feel a pulse are on the inside of the wrist, and on the neck to the side of the windpipe.

The type of activity you are doing can greatly affect the rate of your pulse. Try the experiments below and complete the chart by –

1. counting the number of heart beats in 15 seconds.
2. multiplying that number by 4 to get the pulse rate for one minute.

Study your results. Explain how each type of activity affected your pulse rate.

_____

Activity	Pulse Rate for 15 sec.	X 4 =	Pulse Rate per minute
Sitting still for 10 minutes.			
Running in place for 3 minutes.			
Just after finishing your lunch or dinner.			
While still in bed in the morning.			
Just after getting ready for school.			

Pressure Points

When a person is severely cut and begins to bleed, it's time for quick action. First aid for severe bleeding involves applying pressure over the wound. Sometimes it is possible to press the artery above the wound against the bone behind it, and stop the bleeding. This place is called a **pressure point**. A pressure point is also an excellent location to take a person's pulse.

Place an "X" on the pressure points listed in the Word Bank.

WORD BANK

neck	behind the knee	inside the thigh
wrist	bend of elbow	top of foot

94

Food Pyramid

Your body will get the nutrients it needs if you follow the rules of the food group pyramid. Be sure to make fruits, vegetables, and grains the basic foods of your diet. Eat plenty of healthy foods from the bottom of the pyramid every day.

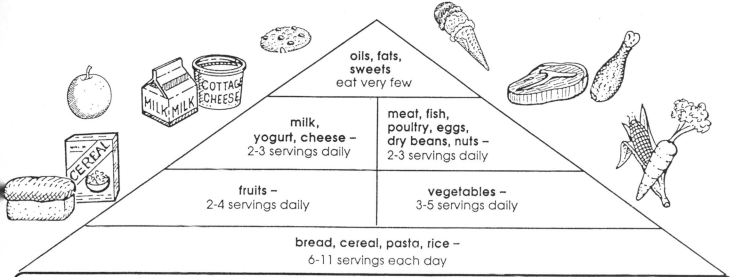

oils, fats, sweets
eat very few

milk, yogurt, cheese –
2-3 servings daily

meat, fish, poultry, eggs, dry beans, nuts –
2-3 servings daily

fruits –
2-4 servings daily

vegetables –
3-5 servings daily

bread, cereal, pasta, rice –
6-11 servings each day

Find Out

What foods do you eat each day? Choose a day and make a chart of what you eat. Record the kind of food and the number of servings.

Group	Breakfast	Lunch	Dinner	Snack
Bread, cereal, pasta, rice				
Vegetables				
Fruits				
Meat, fish, poultry, eggs, dry beans, nuts				
milk, cheese, and yogurt				
Fats, oils, and sweets				

How did you do? Compare your servings with what is indicated on the food pyramid.

95

Snacker's Survey

Do you have a bad case of the munchies, crunchies, or nibbles? Some snack foods can be good for you, while others are terrible. Foods that are lower on the food pyramid are usually much better for you because they contain smaller amounts of fat.

Take a **Snacker's Survey**.

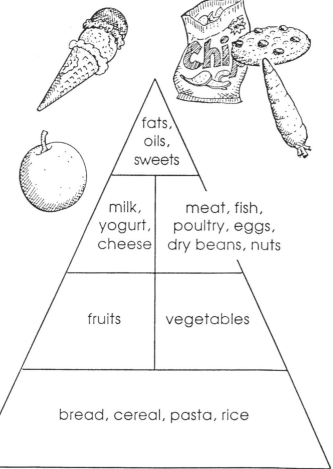

Snacker's Survey

Write the food group to which each snack belongs. Then, using a scale of 1-10, with 1 being the lowest, give each snack a taste score and a nutrition score.

Snack	Food Group	Taste Score	Nutrition Score
Apple			
Cheese			
Cookie			
Potato Chips			
Orange			
Carrot			
Cake			
Candy Bar			
Bagel			
Beef Jerky			
Popcorn			
Pretzels			

Fun Fact!

Labels might not use the name **sugar** when it lists a sweetener. Watch for other names for sugar.

Dextrose	Lactose
Corn Syrup	Fructose
Molasses	Sucrose

Name the Nutrient

Name _____

Your body is made up of millions of cells that need food to stay alive. Your body needs **nutrients** from the foods you eat to help the cells grow and repair themselves. Nutrients are divided into six major groups: **fats, proteins, carbohydrates, minerals, vitamins** and **water.**

Read each clue. Identify the nutrient.

"I'm the body's building material. You need me to make new tissue. You get plenty of me from milk, beans, meat, and peanuts."

Who am I? _____

"I give you energy to work and play. You can find me in starchy foods like pasta and potatoes."

Who am I? _____

"I help build strong bones and teeth. I also give you healthy red blood. You can find me in all four food groups."

Who am I? _____

"I give you a concentrated source of energy. You can find me in oily and greasy foods, like bacon, salad dressing, and butter. I also help you maintain healthy skin and hair."

Who am I? _____

"You might call me the alphabet soup of the nutrients. I am one of the essential nutrients. I don't give you energy, but I do help your body get energy from the other nutrients."

Who am I? _____

"I make up over half of your body weight. My job is to carry all those good nutrients throughout your body. I also help your body to remove wastes."

Who am I? _____

WORD BANK
fat
protein
carbohydrate
water
vitamin
mineral

You Are What You Eat

Looking closely at the information on a cereal box you can learn many interesting things about the product.

Carefully read the information on the illustration of the cereal box. Answer the questions. Compare these answers with the information found on a box of cereal you might eat for breakfast.

	Corn Balls	Your Cereal
What kind of grain(s) is used?		
Is sugar used?		
What position is sugar on the list of ingredients?		
List other sweeteners.		
How many calories per serving without milk?		
How many calories per per serving when eaten with 1/2 cup of skim milk?		
How much protein per serving?		
How many vitamins and minerals does the cereal contain?		
How much cholesterol is in one serving?		
How much fat is in one serving?		
How much carbohydrate is in one serving?		

NUTRITION INFORMATION

SERVING SIZE: 1 OZ. (28.4 g, ABOUT 1 CUP)
CORN BALLS ALONE OR WITH 1/2 CUP
VITAMINS A AND D SKIM MILK.
SERVINGS PER PACKAGE: 15

	CEREAL	WITH 1/2 CUP VITAMINS A & D SKIM MILK
CALORIES	110	150*
PROTEIN	1 g	5 g
CARBOHYDRATE	26 g	32 g
FAT	0 g	0 g*
CHOLESTEROL	0 mg	0 mg*
SODIUM	90 mg	150 mg
POTASSIUM	20 mg	220 mg

PERCENTAGE OF U.S. RECOMMENDED DAILY ALLOWANCES (U.S. RDA)

PROTEIN	2	10
VITAMIN A	15	20
VITAMIN C	25	25
THIAMIN	25	30
RIBOFLAVIN	25	35
NIACIN	25	25
CALCIUM	**	15
IRON	10	10
VITAMIN D	10	25
VITAMIN B$_6$	25	25
ZINC	10	15

* WHOLE MILK SUPPLIES AN ADDITIONAL 30
  CALORIES. 4g. FAT, AND 15mg CHOLESTEROL.
** CONTAINS LESS THAN 2% OF THE U.S. RDA
  OF THIS NUTRIENT.

INGREDIENTS: CORN, SUGAR, CORN SYRUP, MOLASSES, SALT, ANNATTO COLOR,

VITAMINS AND MINERALS: VITAMIN C (SODIUM ASCORBATE AND ASCORBIC ACID), NIACINAMIDE, ZINC (OXIDE), IRON, VITAMIN B6 (PYRIDOXINE HYDROCHLORIDE), VITAMIN B2 (RIBOFLAVIN), VITAMIN A (PALMITATE; PROTECTED WITH BHT), VITAMIN B1 (THIAMIN HYDROCHLORIDE), FOLIC ACID, AND VITAMIN D.

Burning Calories to Stay Healthy

Name _____

Regular exercise makes your heart strong, and it also helps you burn calories so you maintain a healthy weight.

The activities named below list the number of calories burned by a 150-pound person when he or she engages in an activity for 30 minutes. Circle the 10 activities below that help you burn the most calories.

Activity	Calories Burned in 30 Minutes	Activity	Calories Burned in 30 Minutes
cross country skiing	210	homework	55
running (7 mph)	275	racquetball	365
shuffleboard	90	baseball	60
bicycling (stationary)	150	soccer	360
aerobic dancing	200	swimming	265
watching TV	45	tennis	225
walking (5.5 mph)	280	basketball	345

Complete the chart below to keep a record of the exercise you do for one week.

	Type of Exercise	Length of Time (minutes)	Approximate Calories Burned
Sunday			
Monday			
Tuesday			
Wednesday			
Thursday			
Friday			
Saturday			

Reading the Label

The labels on medicine containers give us important information. Labels should always be read carefully.

Read the information on the cough medicine labels below. Answer the questions on the lines provided.

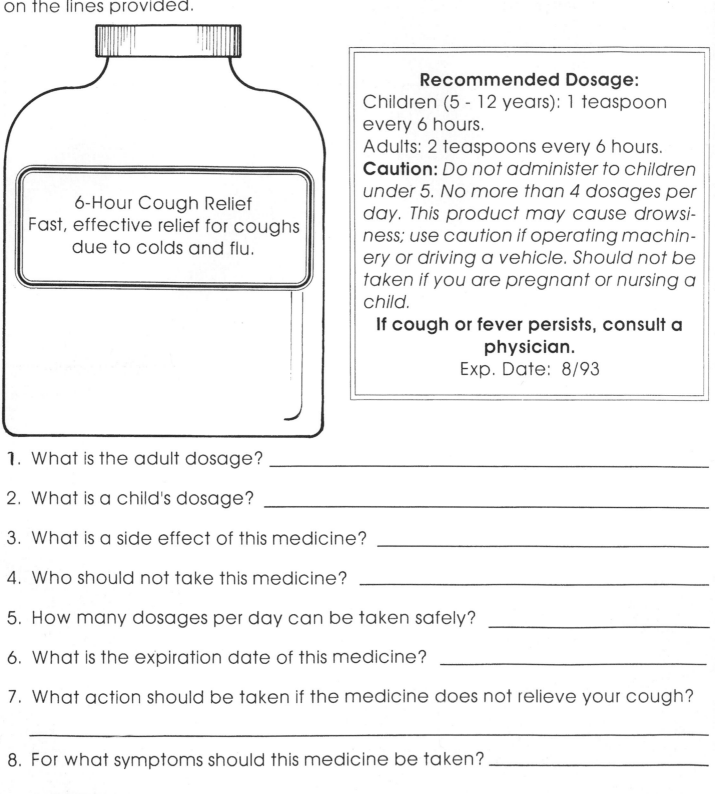

Recommended Dosage:
Children (5 - 12 years): 1 teaspoon every 6 hours.
Adults: 2 teaspoons every 6 hours.
Caution: *Do not administer to children under 5. No more than 4 dosages per day. This product may cause drowsiness; use caution if operating machinery or driving a vehicle. Should not be taken if you are pregnant or nursing a child.*
If cough or fever persists, consult a physician.
Exp. Date: 8/93

6-Hour Cough Relief
Fast, effective relief for coughs due to colds and flu.

1. What is the adult dosage? _____

2. What is a child's dosage? _____

3. What is a side effect of this medicine? _____

4. Who should not take this medicine? _____

5. How many dosages per day can be taken safely? _____

6. What is the expiration date of this medicine? _____

7. What action should be taken if the medicine does not relieve your cough?

_____

8. For what symptoms should this medicine be taken? _____

_____

Caution: Poison!

Children are always very curious. They love to touch things and pick them up. Very young children like to put things into their mouths. What action do you take if a child swallows a poisonous material?

Read the following safety procedures.

CALL YOUR POISON CONTROL CENTER, HOSPITAL, PHYSICIAN, OR EMERGENCY PHONE NUMBER IMMEDIATELY!!

If you cannot obtain emergency advice, follow these procedures.

• If the poison is **corrosive:** paint remover, household cleaners, gasoline, drain opener, ammonia or lye, **DO NOT** make the patient vomit. Give the patient water or milk to dilute the poison.

• If the poison is **not corrosive:** insect spray, aspirin, pesticides or medicine, **make the patient vomit,** or use a poison control kit. To force the patient to vomit touch the back of his/her throat.

Write a bold "**V**" on each picture that shows poison that should be vomited if swallowed. **Circle** each poison that should **not** be vomited if swallowed.

Human Body Review

Name _____

Use the Word Bank to complete the puzzle.

Across:

1. outer layer of skin
4. the blood pump
6. stores urine
10. the "bite" is the _____ of the teeth
11. opening to the uterus
12. boney structure
13. the inside of the hand
14. controls body growth and other glands
17. a break in a bone
20. rhythm of the heart creates a _____
21. female sex glands
22. determine human traits

Down:

1. waste removal system
2. outer layer of the tooth
3. upper arm bone
5. gland that goes to work when we are excited, angry, or frightened
7. fluid surrounding fetus
8. long food tube
9. joint found in elbow
12. oily substance given off by the sebaceous gland
13. gland which controls the body's use of glucose
15. place by or beside a wound to stop bleeding
16. muscles are attached to the skeleton by _____
18. male sex glands
19. framework of bones that supports lower part of abdomen

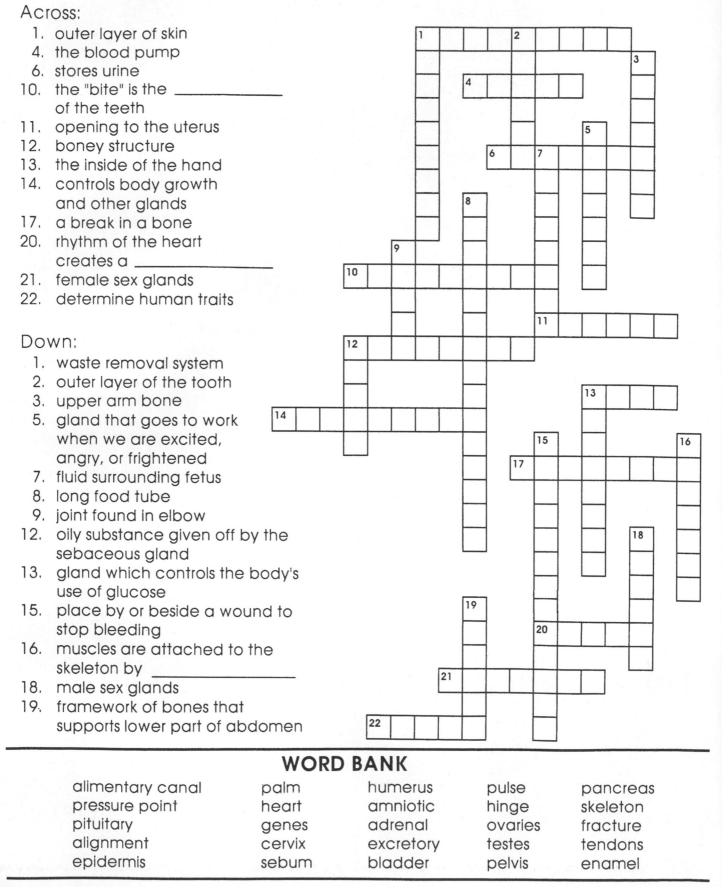

WORD BANK

alimentary canal	palm	humerus	pulse	pancreas
pressure point	heart	amniotic	hinge	skeleton
pituitary	genes	adrenal	ovaries	fracture
alignment	cervix	excretory	testes	tendons
epidermis	sebum	bladder	pelvis	enamel

Answer Key

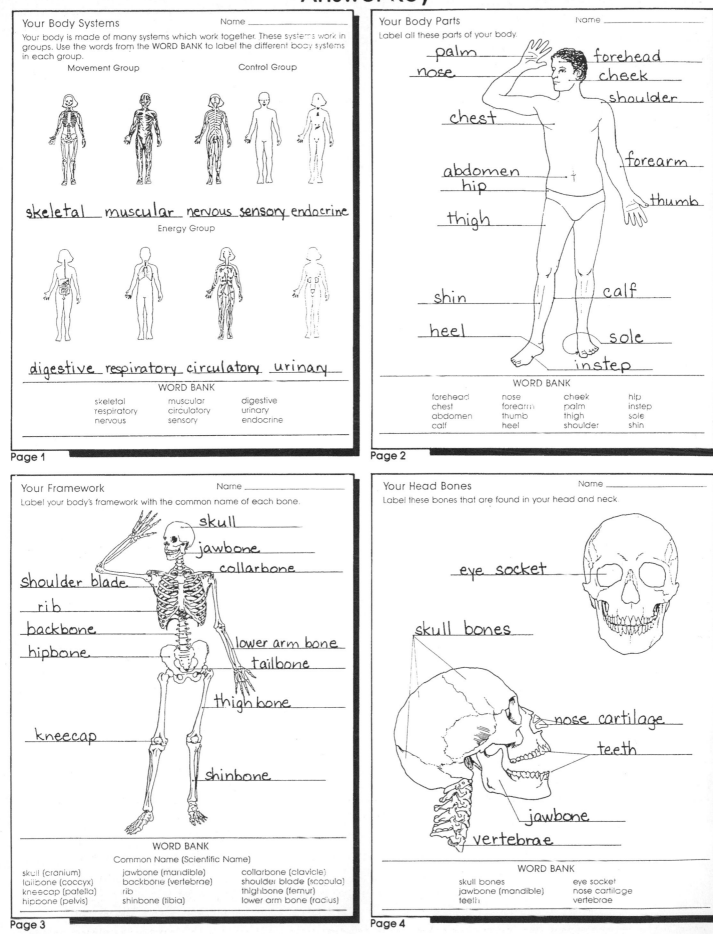

Your Body Systems Name _____

Your body is made of many systems which work together. These systems work in groups. Use the words from the WORD BANK to label the different body systems in each group.

Movement Group   Control Group

skeletal   muscular   nervous   sensory   endocrine

Energy Group

digestive   respiratory   circulatory   urinary

WORD BANK

skeletal	muscular	digestive
respiratory	circulatory	urinary
nervous	sensory	endocrine

Your Body Parts Name _____

Label all these parts of your body.

palm
nose
forehead
cheek
shoulder
chest
forearm
abdomen
hip
thumb
thigh
shin
calf
heel
sole
instep

WORD BANK

forehead	nose	cheek	hip
chest	forearm	palm	instep
abdomen	thumb	thigh	sole
calf	heel	shoulder	shin

Your Framework Name _____

Label your body's framework with the common name of each bone.

skull
jawbone
collarbone
shoulder blade
rib
backbone
hipbone
lower arm bone
tailbone
thigh bone
kneecap
shinbone

WORD BANK
Common Name (Scientific Name)

skull (cranium)	jawbone (mandible)	collarbone (clavicle)
tailbone (coccyx)	backbone (vertebrae)	shoulder blade (scapula)
kneecap (patella)	rib	thighbone (femur)
hipbone (pelvis)	shinbone (tibia)	lower arm bone (radius)

Your Head Bones Name _____

Label these bones that are found in your head and neck.

eye socket
skull bones
nose cartilage
teeth
jawbone
vertebrae

WORD BANK

skull bones	eye socket
jawbone (mandible)	nose cartilage
teeth	vertebrae

Answer Key

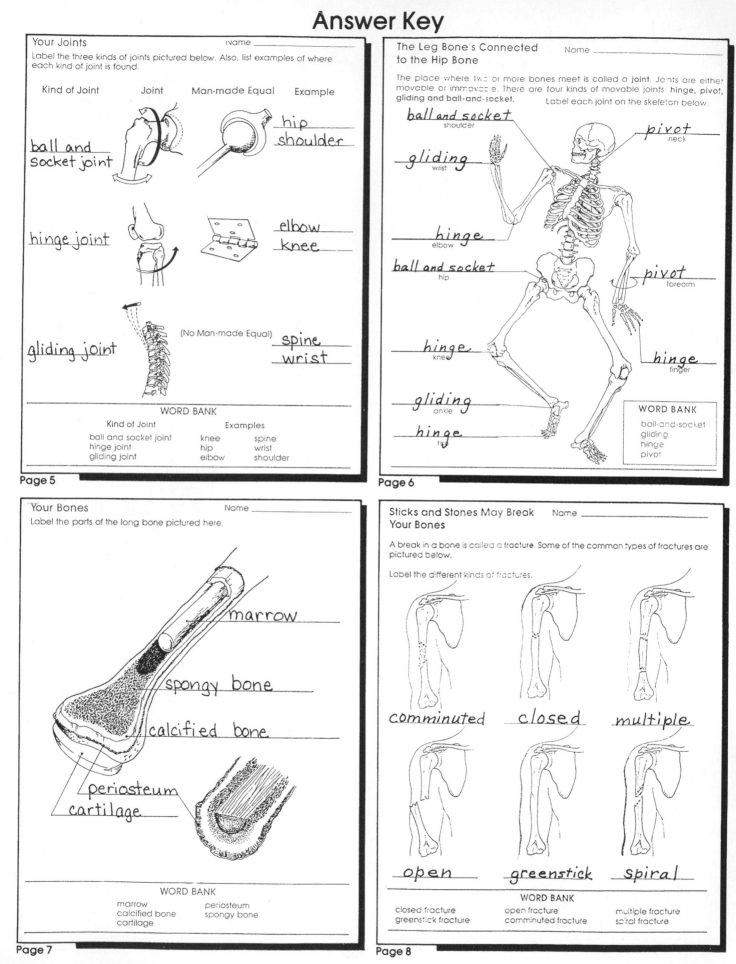

Your Joints

Name _____

Label the three kinds of joints pictured below. Also, list examples of where each kind of joint is found.

Kind of Joint   Joint   Man-made Equal   Example

ball and socket joint

hip
shoulder

hinge joint

elbow
knee

gliding joint

(No Man-made Equal)

spine
wrist

WORD BANK

Kind of Joint	Examples	
ball and socket joint	knee	spine
hinge joint	hip	wrist
gliding joint	elbow	shoulder

Page 5

The Leg Bone's Connected to the Hip Bone

Name _____

The place where two or more bones meet is called a joint. Joints are either movable or immovable. There are four kinds of movable joints: hinge, pivot, gliding and ball-and-socket.   Label each joint on the skeleton below.

ball and socket — shoulder

gliding — wrist

pivot — neck

hinge — elbow

ball and socket — hip

pivot — forearm

hinge — knee

hinge — finger

gliding — ankle

hinge — toe

WORD BANK

ball-and-socket
gliding
hinge
pivot

Page 6

Your Bones

Name _____

Label the parts of the long bone pictured here.

marrow

spongy bone

calcified bone

periosteum

cartilage

WORD BANK

marrow	periosteum
calcified bone	spongy bone
cartilage	

Page 7

Sticks and Stones May Break Your Bones

Name _____

A break in a bone is called a fracture. Some of the common types of fractures are pictured below.

Label the different kinds of fractures.

comminuted   closed   multiple

open   greenstick   spiral

WORD BANK

closed fracture	open fracture	multiple fracture
greenstick fracture	comminuted fracture	spiral fracture

Page 8

The Human Body IF8754   104   © 1990 Instructional Fair, Inc.

Answer Key

Your Backbone
Name _____

Label the regions of your backbone, or vertebral column.

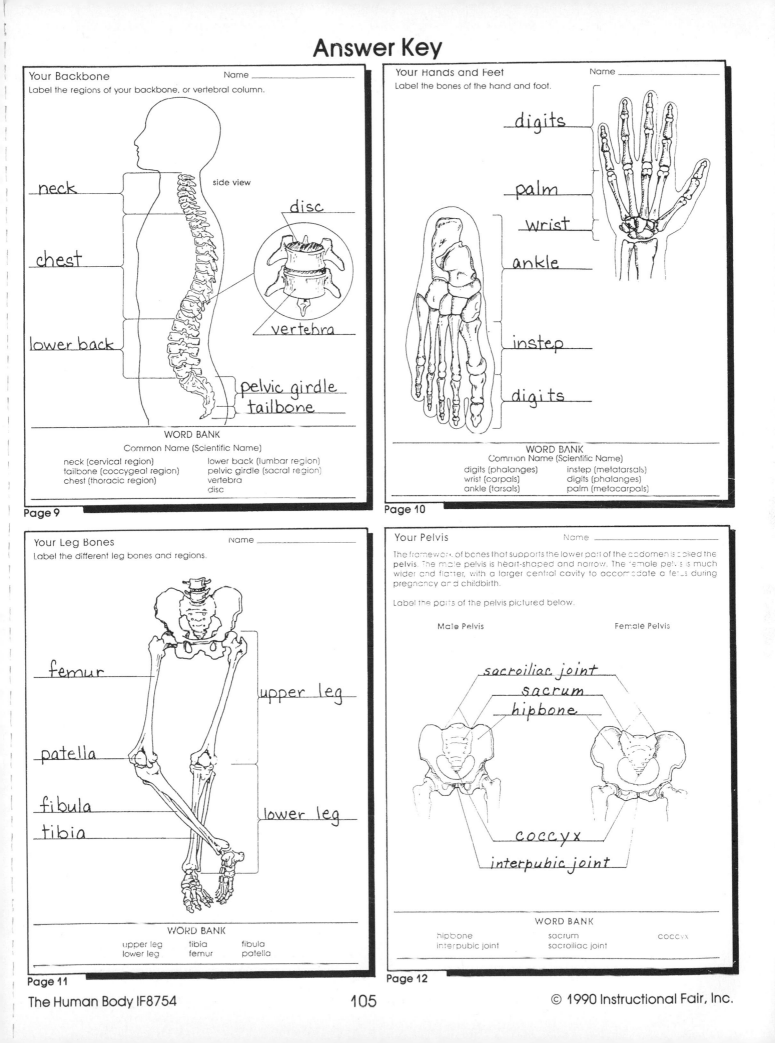

neck

side view

chest

disc

lower back

vertebra

pelvic girdle
tailbone

WORD BANK
Common Name (Scientific Name)

neck (cervical region)
tailbone (coccygeal region)
chest (thoracic region)

lower back (lumbar region)
pelvic girdle (sacral region)
vertebra
disc

Your Hands and Feet
Name _____

Label the bones of the hand and foot.

digits

palm

wrist

ankle

instep

digits

WORD BANK
Common Name (Scientific Name)

digits (phalanges)
wrist (carpals)
ankle (tarsals)

instep (metatarsals)
digits (phalanges)
palm (metacarpals)

Your Leg Bones
Name _____

Label the different leg bones and regions.

femur

upper leg

patella

fibula
tibia

lower leg

WORD BANK

upper leg   tibia   fibula
lower leg   femur   patella

Your Pelvis
Name _____

The framework of bones that supports the lower part of the abdomen is called the pelvis. The male pelvis is heart-shaped and narrow. The female pelvis is much wider and flatter, with a larger central cavity to accommodate a fetus during pregnancy and childbirth.

Label the parts of the pelvis pictured below.

Male Pelvis   Female Pelvis

sacroiliac joint
sacrum
hipbone

coccyx
interpubic joint

WORD BANK

hipbone   sacrum   coccyx
interpubic joint   sacroiliac joint

Answer Key

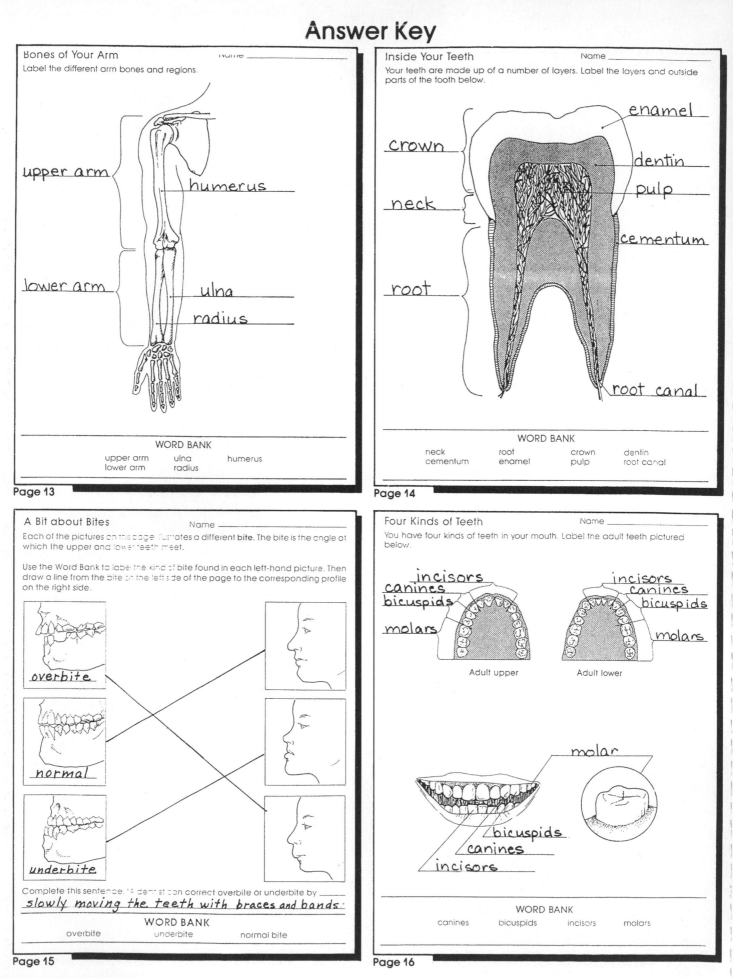

Bones of Your Arm
Name _____
Label the different arm bones and regions.

upper arm
humerus
lower arm
ulna
radius

WORD BANK

upper arm	ulna	humerus
lower arm	radius	

Page 13

Inside Your Teeth
Name _____
Your teeth are made up of a number of layers. Label the layers and outside parts of the tooth below.

enamel
crown
dentin
pulp
neck
cementum
root
root canal

WORD BANK

neck	root	crown	dentin
cementum	enamel	pulp	root canal

Page 14

A Bit about Bites
Name _____

Each of the pictures on this page illustrates a different **bite**. The bite is the angle at which the upper and lower teeth meet.

Use the Word Bank to label the kind of bite found in each left-hand picture. Then draw a line from the bite on the left side of the page to the corresponding profile on the right side.

overbite

normal

underbite

Complete this sentence: A dentist can correct overbite or underbite by _____
slowly moving the teeth with braces and bands.

WORD BANK

overbite	underbite	normal bite

Page 15

Four Kinds of Teeth
Name _____
You have four kinds of teeth in your mouth. Label the adult teeth pictured below.

incisors
canines
bicuspids
molars

incisors
canines
bicuspids
molars

Adult upper   Adult lower

molar

bicuspids
canines
incisors

WORD BANK

canines	bicuspids	incisors	molars

Page 16

Answer Key

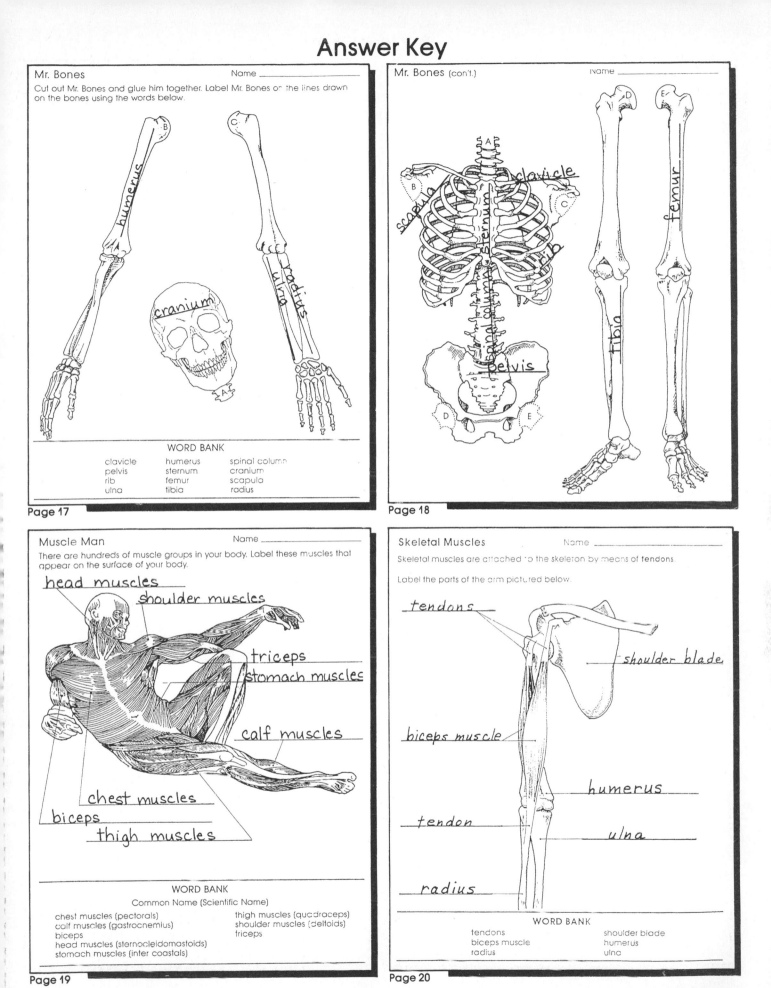

Mr. Bones   Name _____

Cut out Mr. Bones and glue him together. Label Mr. Bones on the lines drawn on the bones using the words below.

humerus B

radius C

cranium

ulna

WORD BANK

clavicle	humerus	spinal column
pelvis	sternum	cranium
rib	femur	scapula
ulna	tibia	radius

Page 17

Mr. Bones (con't.)   Name _____

D   E

scapula B   *clavicle*

spinal column   *sternum*   C

rib

pelvis

femur

tibia

D   E

Page 18

Muscle Man   Name _____

There are hundreds of muscle groups in your body. Label these muscles that appear on the surface of your body.

head muscles

shoulder muscles

triceps

stomach muscles

calf muscles

chest muscles

biceps

thigh muscles

WORD BANK

Common Name (Scientific Name)

chest muscles (pectorals)	thigh muscles (quadraceps)
calf muscles (gastrocnemius)	shoulder muscles (deltoids)
biceps	triceps
head muscles (sternocleidomastoids)	
stomach muscles (inter coastals)	

Page 19

Skeletal Muscles   Name _____

Skeletal muscles are attached to the skeleton by means of **tendons**.

Label the parts of the arm pictured below.

tendons

shoulder blade

biceps muscle

humerus

tendon

ulna

radius

WORD BANK

tendons	shoulder blade
biceps muscle	humerus
radius	ulna

Page 20

The Human Body IF8754   107   © 1990 Instructional Fair, Inc.

Answer Key

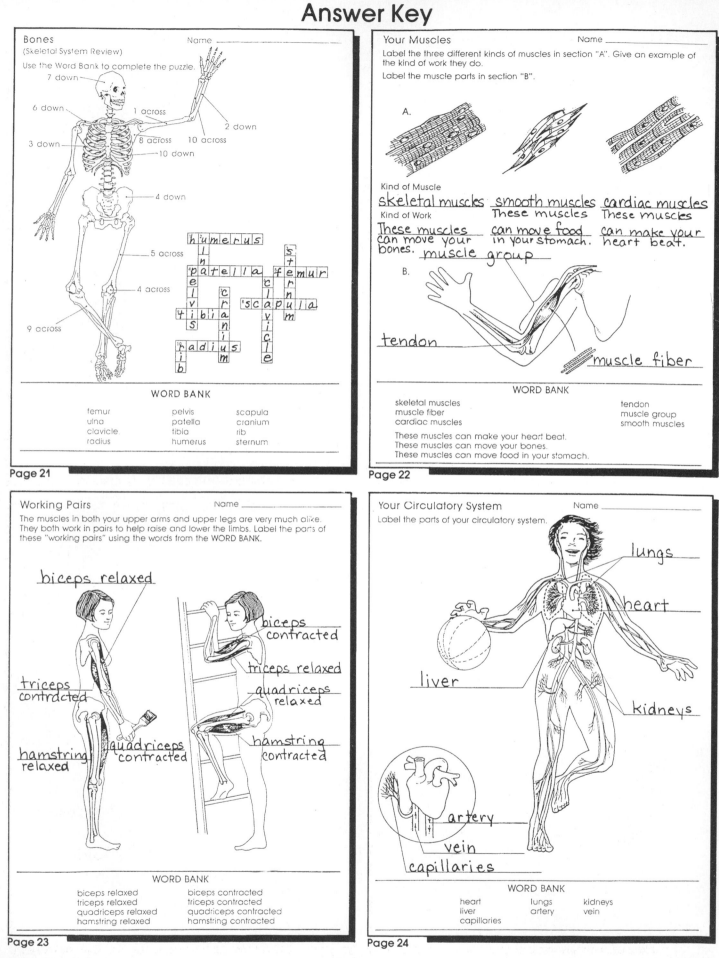

Bones
(Skeletal System Review)   Name _____

Use the Word Bank to complete the puzzle.

7 down
6 down   1 across
              2 down
3 down   8 across   10 across
          10 down
                      4 down

— 5 across
— 4 across
9 across

Crossword answers:
h u m e r u s
p a t e l l a   f e m u r
t i b i a   s c a p u l a
r a d i u s

(letters visible in puzzle: humerus, patella, femur, pelvis, cranium, clavicle, sternum, tibia, scapula, radius, rib)

WORD BANK

femur	pelvis	scapula
ulna	patella	cranium
clavicle	tibia	rib
radius	humerus	sternum

Your Muscles   Name _____

Label the three different kinds of muscles in section "A". Give an example of the kind of work they do.
Label the muscle parts in section "B".

A.

Kind of Muscle
skeletal muscles   smooth muscles   cardiac muscles
Kind of Work   These muscles   These muscles
These muscles   can move food   can make your
can move your   in your stomach. heart beat.
bones.   muscle group

B.
tendon
muscle fiber

WORD BANK

skeletal muscles	tendon
muscle fiber	muscle group
cardiac muscles	smooth muscles

These muscles can make your heart beat.
These muscles can move your bones.
These muscles can move food in your stomach.

Working Pairs   Name _____

The muscles in both your upper arms and upper legs are very much alike. They both work in pairs to help raise and lower the limbs. Label the parts of these "working pairs" using the words from the WORD BANK.

biceps relaxed
biceps contracted
triceps relaxed
triceps contracted
quadriceps relaxed
quadriceps contracted
hamstring relaxed
hamstring contracted

WORD BANK

biceps relaxed	biceps contracted
triceps relaxed	triceps contracted
quadriceps relaxed	quadriceps contracted
hamstring relaxed	hamstring contracted

Your Circulatory System   Name _____

Label the parts of your circulatory system.

lungs
heart
liver
kidneys
artery
vein
capillaries

WORD BANK

heart	lungs	kidneys
liver	artery	vein
capillaries		

Page 21

Page 22

Page 23

Page 24

Answer Key

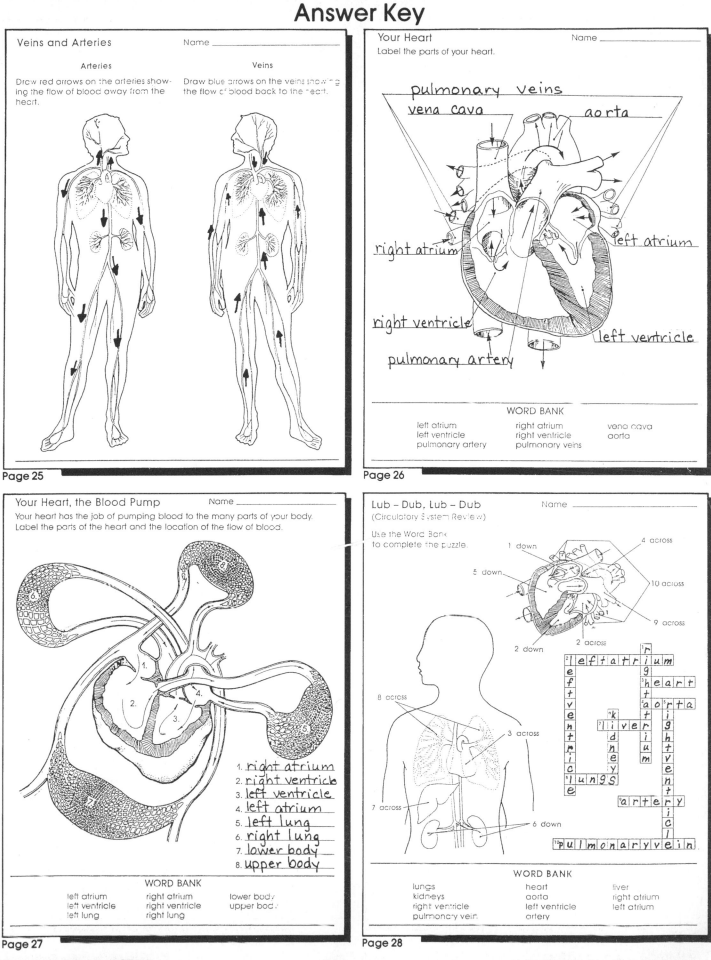

Veins and Arteries   Name _____

Arteries
Draw red arrows on the arteries showing the flow of blood away from the heart.

Veins
Draw blue arrows on the veins showing the flow of blood back to the heart.

Your Heart   Name _____
Label the parts of your heart.

pulmonary veins
vena cava
aorta
right atrium
left atrium
right ventricle
left ventricle
pulmonary artery

WORD BANK

left atrium	right atrium	vena cava
left ventricle	right ventricle	aorta
pulmonary artery	pulmonary veins	

Your Heart, the Blood Pump   Name _____

Your heart has the job of pumping blood to the many parts of your body. Label the parts of the heart and the location of the flow of blood.

1. right atrium
2. right ventricle
3. left ventricle
4. left atrium
5. left lung
6. right lung
7. lower body
8. upper body

WORD BANK

left atrium	right atrium	lower body
left ventricle	right ventricle	upper body
left lung	right lung	

Lub – Dub, Lub – Dub   Name _____
(Circulatory System Review)

Use the Word Bank to complete the puzzle.

1 down
4 across
5 down
10 across
9 across
2 down
2 across
8 across
3 across
7 across
6 down

Crossword answers:
²left atrium
³heart
aorta
⁷liver
⁸lungs
⁹artery
¹⁰pulmonary vein

WORD BANK

lungs	heart	liver
kidneys	aorta	right atrium
right ventricle	left ventricle	left atrium
pulmonary vein	artery	

The Human Body IF8754   109   © 1990 Instructional Fair, Inc.

Answer Key

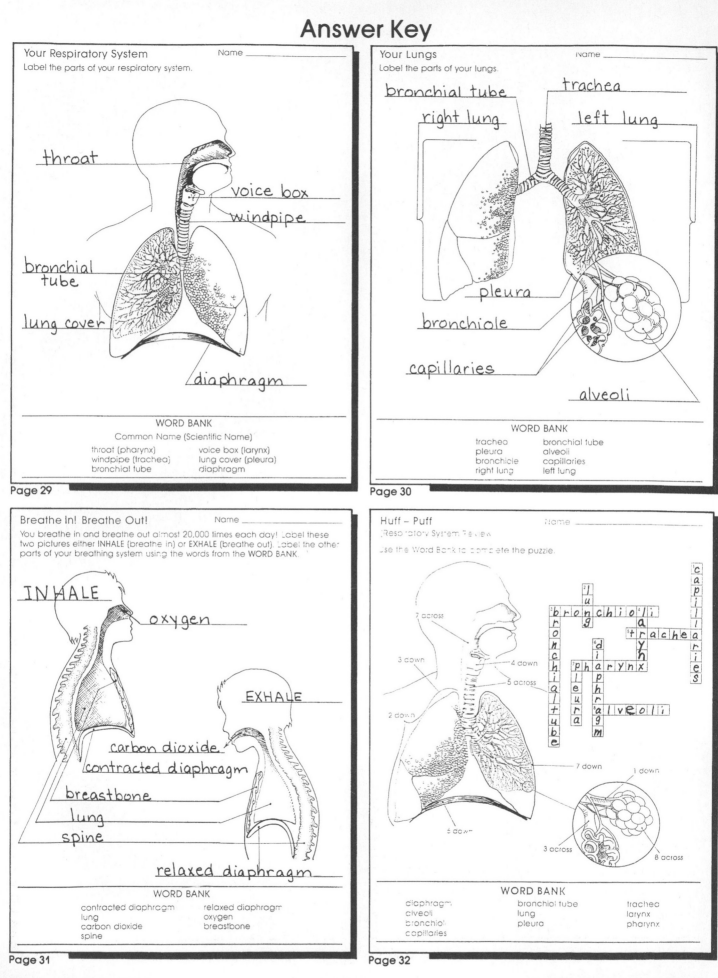

Your Respiratory System

Name _____

Label the parts of your respiratory system.

- throat
- voice box
- windpipe
- bronchial tube
- lung cover
- diaphragm

WORD BANK
Common Name (Scientific Name)

throat (pharynx)	voice box (larynx)
windpipe (trachea)	lung cover (pleura)
bronchial tube	diaphragm

Page 29

Your Lungs

Name _____

Label the parts of your lungs.

- bronchial tube
- trachea
- right lung
- left lung
- pleura
- bronchiole
- capillaries
- alveoli

WORD BANK

trachea	bronchial tube
pleura	alveoli
bronchiole	capillaries
right lung	left lung

Page 30

Breathe In! Breathe Out!

Name _____

You breathe in and breathe out almost 20,000 times each day! Label these two pictures either INHALE (breathe in) or EXHALE (breathe out). Label the other parts of your breathing system using the words from the WORD BANK.

- INHALE
- oxygen
- EXHALE
- carbon dioxide
- contracted diaphragm
- breastbone
- lung
- spine
- relaxed diaphragm

WORD BANK

contracted diaphragm	relaxed diaphragm
lung	oxygen
carbon dioxide	breastbone
spine	

Page 31

Huff – Puff

Name _____

Respiratory System Review

Use the Word Bank to complete the puzzle.

- 7 across
- 3 down
- 4 down
- 5 across
- 2 down
- 7 down
- 1 down
- 6 down
- 3 across
- 8 across

WORD BANK

diaphragm	bronchial tube	trachea
alveoli	lung	larynx
bronchiole	pleura	pharynx
capillaries		

Page 32

The Human Body IF8754   110   © 1990 Instructional Fair, Inc.

Answer Key

Your Digestive System

Name _____

Label the parts of your digestive system.

- teeth
- mouth
- salivary glands
- esophagus
- liver
- stomach
- gall bladder
- pancreas
- large intestine
- small intestine
- anus

WORD BANK

pancreas	liver	gall bladder
stomach	mouth	large intestine
esophagus	teeth	small intestine
salivary glands	anus	

The Alimentary Canal

Name _____

The main part of the digestive system is the **alimentary canal**, a tube which starts at the mouth, and travels through the body ending at the anus. Label the parts of the alimentary canal.

Food enters.

- mouth
- esophagus
- stomach

Bile enters from the liver.

Enzymes enter from the pancreas.

Proteins, fats, vitamins, minerals, and carbohydrates are absorbed into the blood stream.

- small intestine

Water goes into the bloodstream.

- anus

Solid wastes exit.

- large intestine

WORD BANK

anus	small intestine	esophagus
mouth	large intestine	stomach

The Stomach

Name _____

The **stomach** is the widest part of the alimentary canal. The stomach has three layers of muscles which allow it to contract in different directions. The contracting motion mashes food and mixes it with digestive juices.

Label the parts of the stomach and the tubes leading into and out of the stomach.

- esophagus
- muscle layers
- sphincter
- duodenum
- mucous membrane

WORD BANK

sphincter	duodenum	mucous membrane
muscle layers	esophagus	

Digestion in the Mouth

Name _____

Label the parts of the digestive system located in and around the mouth.

- palate
- teeth
- tongue
- salivary glands
- pharynx
- epiglottis
- esophagus

WORD BANK

teeth	tongue	palate
epiglottis	esophagus	salivary glands
pharynx		

The Human Body IF8754   111   © 1990 Instructional Fair, Inc.

Answer Key

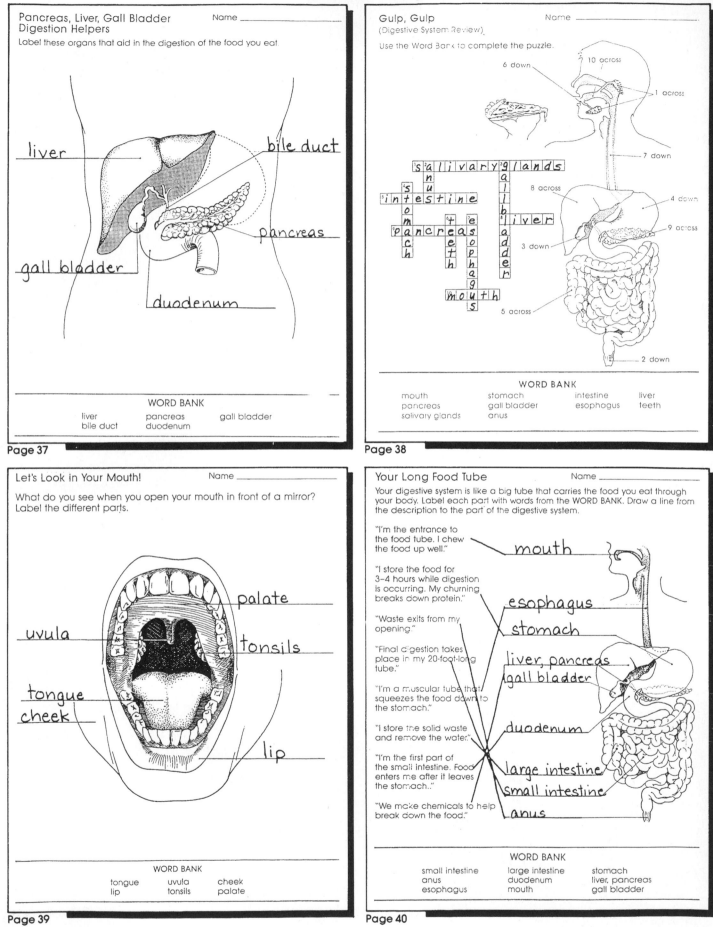

Pancreas, Liver, Gall Bladder
Digestion Helpers

Name _____

Label these organs that aid in the digestion of the food you eat.

liver

bile duct

pancreas

gall bladder

duodenum

WORD BANK

liver   pancreas   gall bladder
bile duct   duodenum

Gulp, Gulp
(Digestive System Review)

Name _____

Use the Word Bank to complete the puzzle.

6 down · 10 across · 1 across · 7 down · 8 across · 4 down · 9 across · 3 down · 5 across · 2 down

Across/Down answers:
salivary glands · intestine · pancreas · liver · mouth
(down words: snout/s-n-u-o-m-a-c-h, gallbladder, teeth, esophagus)

WORD BANK

mouth   stomach   intestine   liver
pancreas   gall bladder   esophagus   teeth
salivary glands   anus

Let's Look in Your Mouth!

Name _____

What do you see when you open your mouth in front of a mirror?
Label the different parts.

palate

uvula

tonsils

tongue

cheek

lip

WORD BANK

tongue   uvula   cheek
lip   tonsils   palate

Your Long Food Tube

Name _____

Your digestive system is like a big tube that carries the food you eat through your body. Label each part with words from the WORD BANK. Draw a line from the description to the part of the digestive system.

"I'm the entrance to the food tube. I chew the food up well."

"I store the food for 3-4 hours while digestion is occurring. My churning breaks down protein."

"Waste exits from my opening."

"Final digestion takes place in my 20-foot-long tube."

"I'm a muscular tube that squeezes the food down to the stomach."

"I store the solid waste and remove the water."

"I'm the first part of the small intestine. Food enters me after it leaves the stomach."

"We make chemicals to help break down the food."

mouth

esophagus

stomach

liver, pancreas

gall bladder

duodenum

large intestine

small intestine

anus

WORD BANK

small intestine   large intestine   stomach
anus   duodenum   liver, pancreas
esophagus   mouth   gall bladder

The Human Body IF8754   112   © 1990 Instructional Fair, Inc.

Answer Key

Blood Scrubbers
Name _____

Label the different parts of your body's urinary system.

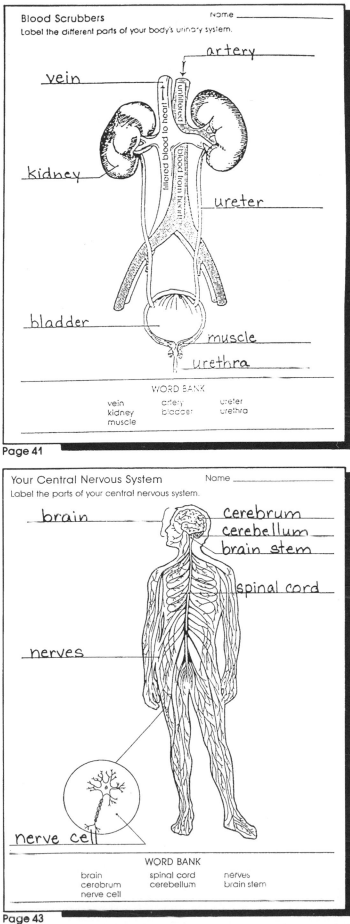

- artery
- vein
- kidney
- ureter
- bladder
- muscle
- urethra

(diagram labels: unfiltered blood to heart, filtered blood from heart)

WORD BANK
vein	artery	ureter
kidney	bladder	urethra
muscle		

Page 41

Waste Removal
Name _____

The important job of removing bodily wastes is performed by the skin and the organs of the urinary and respiratory systems.

Label the excretory organs.

- skin
- kidneys
- lungs
- ureter
- bladder
- urethra

WORD BANK
- skin
- lungs
- urethra
- kidneys
- ureter
- bladder

Complete this chart.

Function	Excretory Organs			
	kidneys	lungs	skin	bladder
removes water	✓	✓	✓	
brings oxygen to blood		✓		
removes salt	✓		✓	
stores urine				✓
removes carbon dioxide		✓		
produces urine	✓			
removes body heat		✓	✓	

Page 42

Your Central Nervous System
Name _____

Label the parts of your central nervous system.

- brain
- cerebrum
- cerebellum
- brain stem
- spinal cord
- nerves
- nerve cell

WORD BANK
brain	spinal cord	nerves
cerebrum	cerebellum	brain stem
nerve cell		

Page 43

Neurons
Name _____

Label the parts of a neuron.

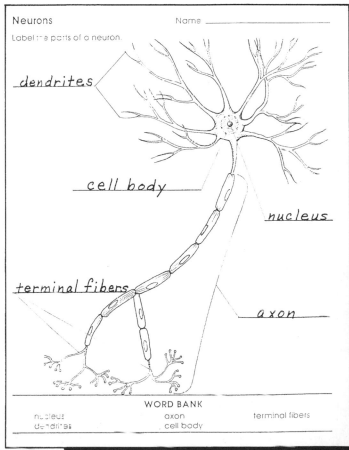

- dendrites
- cell body
- nucleus
- terminal fibers
- axon

WORD BANK
nucleus	axon	terminal fibers
dendrites	cell body	

Page 44

Answer Key

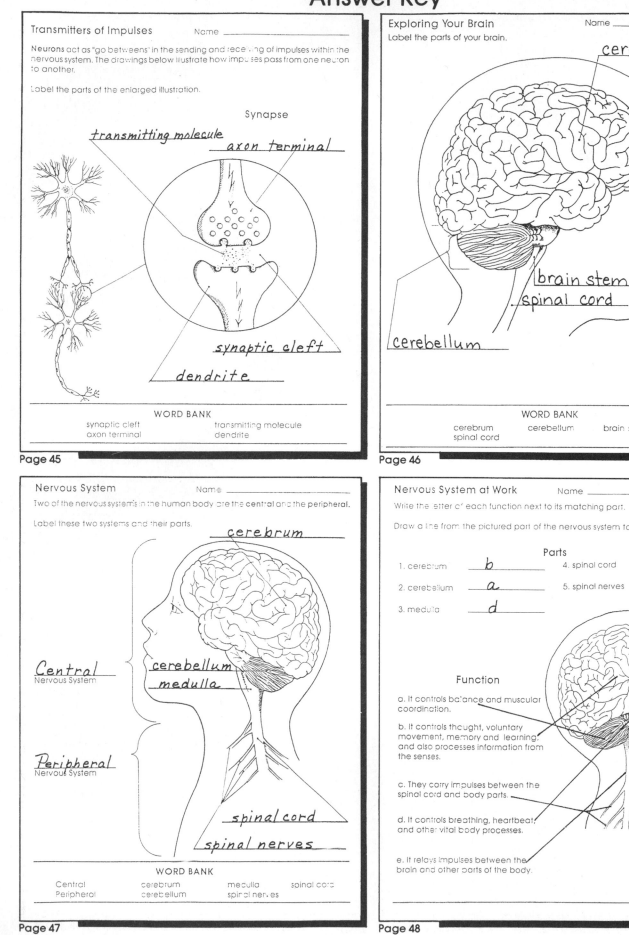

Transmitters of Impulses   Name _____

Neurons act as "go betweens" in the sending and receiving of impulses within the nervous system. The drawings below illustrate how impulses pass from one neuron to another.

Label the parts of the enlarged illustration.

Synapse

transmitting molecule
axon terminal

synaptic cleft

dendrite

WORD BANK
synaptic cleft   transmitting molecule
axon terminal   dendrite

Page 45

Exploring Your Brain   Name _____
Label the parts of your brain.

cerebrum

brain stem
spinal cord

cerebellum

WORD BANK
cerebrum   cerebellum   brain stem
spinal cord

Page 46

Nervous System   Name _____

Two of the nervous systems in the human body are the central and the peripheral.

Label these two systems and their parts.

cerebrum

Central
Nervous System

cerebellum
medulla

Peripheral
Nervous System

spinal cord

spinal nerves

WORD BANK
Central   cerebrum   medulla   spinal cord
Peripheral   cerebellum   spinal nerves

Page 47

Nervous System at Work   Name _____

Write the letter of each function next to its matching part.

Draw a line from the pictured part of the nervous system to its function.

Parts
1. cerebrum   _b_   4. spinal cord   _e_

2. cerebellum   _a_   5. spinal nerves   _c_

3. medulla   _d_

Function

a. It controls balance and muscular coordination.

b. It controls thought, voluntary movement, memory and learning, and also processes information from the senses.

c. They carry impulses between the spinal cord and body parts.

d. It controls breathing, heartbeat, and other vital body processes.

e. It relays impulses between the brain and other parts of the body.

Page 48

The Human Body IF8754   114   © 1990 Instructional Fair, Inc.

Answer Key

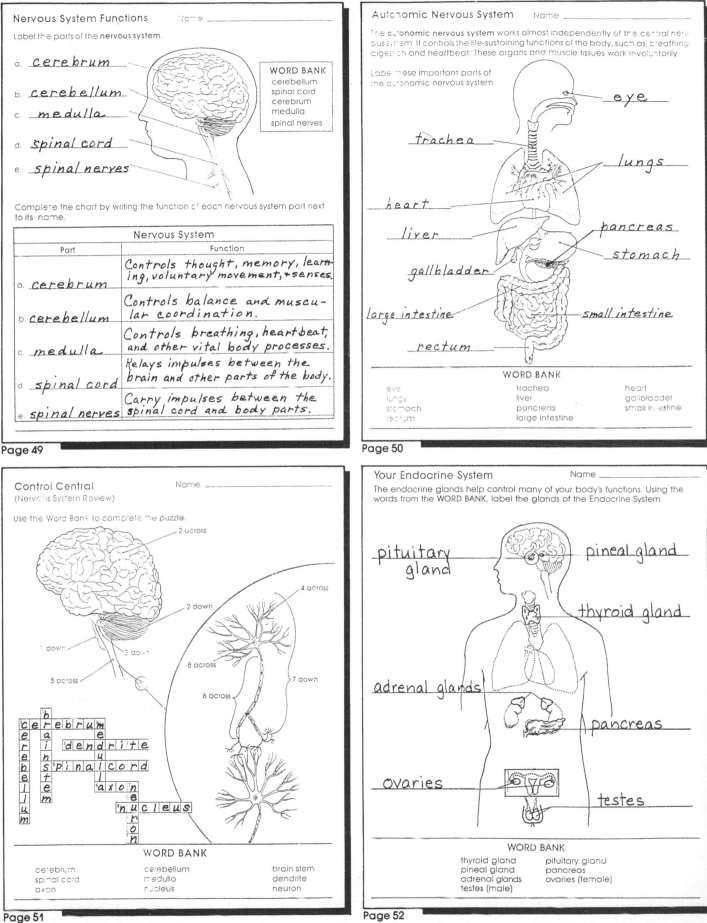

Nervous System Functions
Name _____

Label the parts of the nervous system.

a. *cerebrum*

b. *cerebellum*

c. *medulla*

d. *spinal cord*

e. *spinal nerves*

WORD BANK
cerebellum
spinal cord
cerebrum
medulla
spinal nerves

Complete the chart by writing the function of each nervous system part next to its name.

Nervous System	
Part	Function
a. *cerebrum*	*Controls thought, memory, learning, voluntary movement, + senses.*
b. *cerebellum*	*Controls balance and muscular coordination.*
c. *medulla*	*Controls breathing, heartbeat, and other vital body processes.*
d. *spinal cord*	*Relays impulses between the brain and other parts of the body.*
e. *spinal nerves*	*Carry impulses between the spinal cord and body parts.*

Page 49

Autonomic Nervous System
Name _____

The autonomic nervous system works almost independently of the central nervous system. It controls the life-sustaining functions of the body, such as, breathing, digestion and heartbeat. These organs and muscle tissues work involuntarily.

Label these important parts of the autonomic nervous system.

eye

trachea

lungs

heart

liver

pancreas

stomach

gallbladder

large intestine

small intestine

rectum

WORD BANK
eye
lungs
stomach
rectum
trachea
liver
pancreas
large intestine
heart
gallbladder
small intestine

Page 50

Control Central
(Nervous System Review)

Name _____

Use the Word Bank to complete the puzzle.

2 across
4 across
2 down
1 down
3 down
8 across
5 across
7 down
6 across

c e r e b r u m
e
r
e
b
e
l
l
u
m

b
a
i
n
s
t
e
m

d e n d r i t e
u

s p i n a l c o r d
l

a x o n
e

n u c l e u s
r
o
n

WORD BANK
cerebrum
spinal cord
axon
cerebellum
medulla
nucleus
brain stem
dendrite
neuron

Page 51

Your Endocrine System
Name _____

The endocrine glands help control many of your body's functions. Using the words from the WORD BANK, label the glands of the Endocrine System.

pituitary gland

pineal gland

thyroid gland

adrenal glands

pancreas

ovaries

testes

WORD BANK
thyroid gland
pineal gland
adrenal glands
testes (male)
pituitary gland
pancreas
ovaries (female)

Page 52

Answer Key

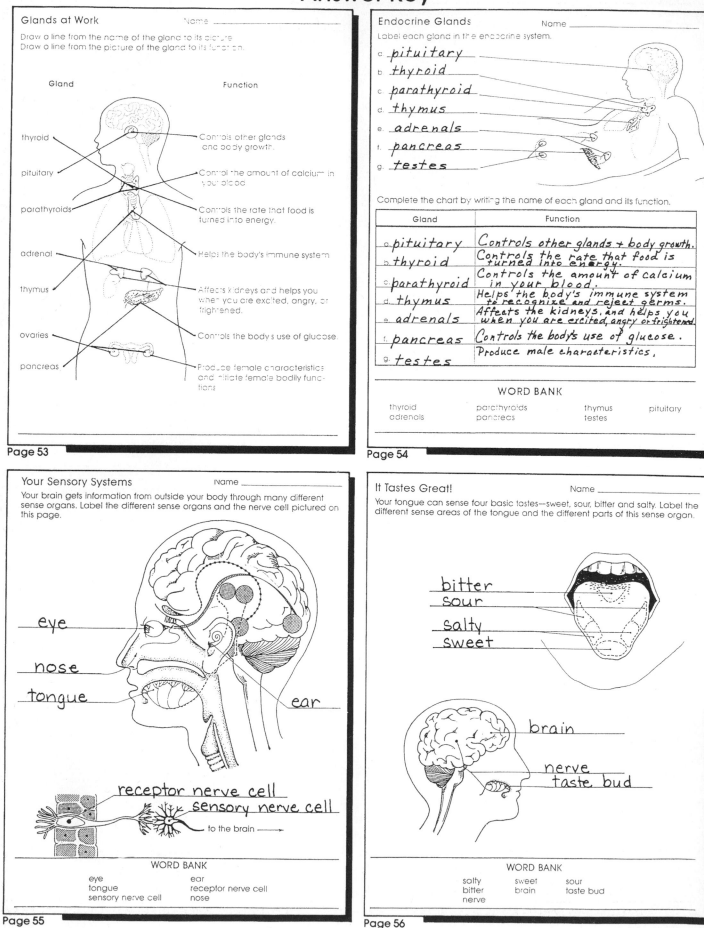

Glands at Work
Name _____

Draw a line from the name of the gland to its picture.
Draw a line from the picture of the gland to its function.

Gland | Function

thyroid

pituitary

parathyroids

adrenal

thymus

ovaries

pancreas

Controls other glands and body growth.

Control the amount of calcium in your blood.

Controls the rate that food is turned into energy.

Helps the body's immune system.

Affects kidneys and helps you when you are excited, angry, or frightened.

Controls the body's use of glucose.

Produce female characteristics and initiate female bodily functions.

Endocrine Glands
Name _____

Label each gland in the endocrine system.

a. *pituitary*
b. *thyroid*
c. *parathyroid*
d. *thymus*
e. *adrenals*
f. *pancreas*
g. *testes*

Complete the chart by writing the name of each gland and its function.

Gland	Function
a. *pituitary*	*Controls other glands + body growth.*
b. *thyroid*	*Controls the rate that food is turned into energy.*
c. *parathyroid*	*Controls the amount of calcium in your blood.*
d. *thymus*	*Helps the body's immune system to recognize and reject germs.*
e. *adrenals*	*Affects the kidneys, and helps you when you are excited, angry or frightened.*
f. *pancreas*	*Controls the body's use of glucose.*
g. *testes*	*Produce male characteristics.*

WORD BANK

thyroid	parathyroids	thymus	pituitary
adrenals	pancreas	testes	

Your Sensory Systems
Name _____

Your brain gets information from outside your body through many different sense organs. Label the different sense organs and the nerve cell pictured on this page.

eye

nose

tongue

ear

receptor nerve cell
sensory nerve cell
to the brain ———>

WORD BANK

eye	ear
tongue	receptor nerve cell
sensory nerve cell	nose

It Tastes Great!
Name _____

Your tongue can sense four basic tastes—sweet, sour, bitter and salty. Label the different sense areas of the tongue and the different parts of this sense organ.

bitter
sour

salty
sweet

brain

nerve
taste bud

WORD BANK

salty	sweet	sour
bitter	brain	taste bud
nerve		

Answer Key

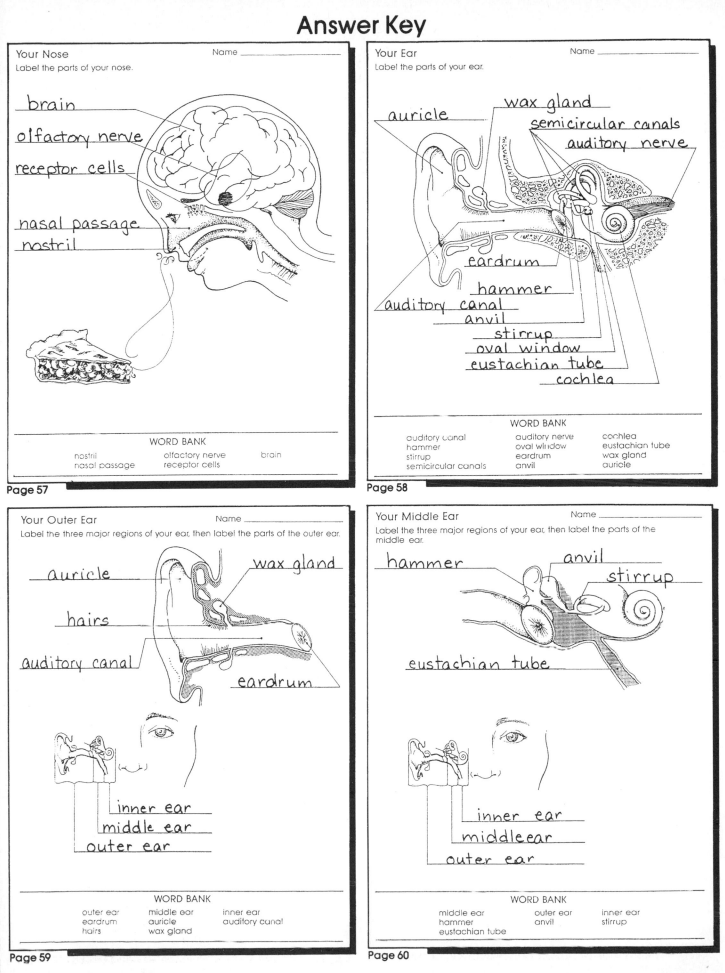

Your Nose   Name _____

Label the parts of your nose.

brain

olfactory nerve

receptor cells

nasal passage

nostril

WORD BANK

nostril	olfactory nerve	brain
nasal passage	receptor cells	

Page 57

Your Ear   Name _____

Label the parts of your ear.

auricle

wax gland

semicircular canals

auditory nerve

eardrum

hammer

auditory canal

anvil

stirrup

oval window

eustachian tube

cochlea

WORD BANK

auditory canal	auditory nerve	cochlea
hammer	oval window	eustachian tube
stirrup	eardrum	wax gland
semicircular canals	anvil	auricle

Page 58

Your Outer Ear   Name _____

Label the three major regions of your ear, then label the parts of the outer ear.

auricle

wax gland

hairs

auditory canal

eardrum

inner ear

middle ear

outer ear

WORD BANK

outer ear	middle ear	inner ear
eardrum	auricle	auditory canal
hairs	wax gland	

Page 59

Your Middle Ear   Name _____

Label the three major regions of your ear, then label the parts of the middle ear.

hammer

anvil

stirrup

eustachian tube

inner ear

middle ear

outer ear

WORD BANK

middle ear	outer ear	inner ear
hammer	anvil	stirrup
eustachian tube		

Page 60

Answer Key

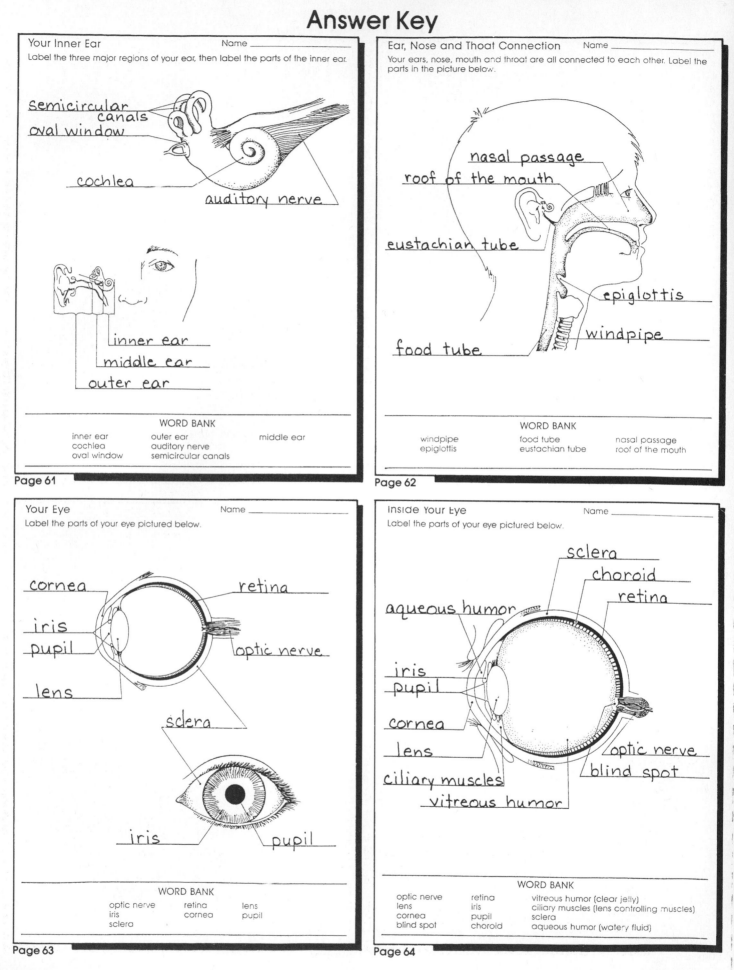

Your Inner Ear
Name _____

Label the three major regions of your ear, then label the parts of the inner ear.

semicircular canals
oval window
cochlea
auditory nerve

inner ear
middle ear
outer ear

WORD BANK
inner ear	outer ear	middle ear
cochlea	auditory nerve	
oval window	semicircular canals	

Page 61

Ear, Nose and Thoat Connection
Name _____

Your ears, nose, mouth and throat are all connected to each other. Label the parts in the picture below.

nasal passage
roof of the mouth
eustachian tube
epiglottis
windpipe
food tube

WORD BANK
windpipe	food tube	nasal passage
epiglottis	eustachian tube	roof of the mouth

Page 62

Your Eye
Name _____

Label the parts of your eye pictured below.

cornea
retina
iris
pupil
optic nerve
lens
sclera
iris
pupil

WORD BANK
optic nerve	retina	lens
iris	cornea	pupil
sclera		

Page 63

Inside Your Eye
Name _____

Label the parts of your eye pictured below.

sclera
choroid
retina
aqueous humor
iris
pupil
cornea
lens
optic nerve
ciliary muscles
blind spot
vitreous humor

WORD BANK
optic nerve	retina	vitreous humor (clear jelly)
lens	iris	ciliary muscles (lens controlling muscles)
cornea	pupil	sclera
blind spot	choroid	aqueous humor (watery fluid)

Page 64

Answer Key

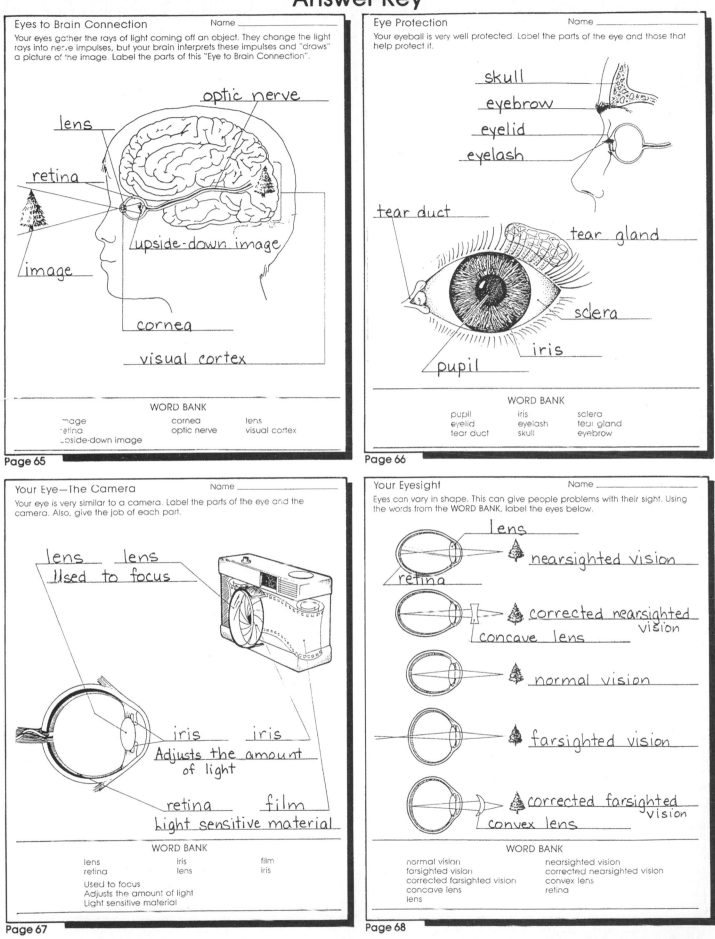

Eyes to Brain Connection   Name _____

Your eyes gather the rays of light coming off an object. They change the light rays into nerve impulses, but your brain interprets these impulses and "draws" a picture of the image. Label the parts of this "Eye to Brain Connection".

- optic nerve
- lens
- retina
- upside-down image
- image
- cornea
- visual cortex

WORD BANK

image	cornea	lens
retina	optic nerve	visual cortex
upside-down image		

Page 65

Eye Protection   Name _____

Your eyeball is very well protected. Label the parts of the eye and those that help protect it.

- skull
- eyebrow
- eyelid
- eyelash
- tear duct
- tear gland
- sclera
- iris
- pupil

WORD BANK

pupil	iris	sclera
eyelid	eyelash	tear gland
tear duct	skull	eyebrow

Page 66

Your Eye—The Camera   Name _____

Your eye is very similar to a camera. Label the parts of the eye and the camera. Also, give the job of each part.

- lens   lens
- Used to focus
- iris   iris
- Adjusts the amount of light
- retina   film
- Light sensitive material

WORD BANK

lens	iris	film
retina	lens	iris

Used to focus
Adjusts the amount of light
Light sensitive material

Page 67

Your Eyesight   Name _____

Eyes can vary in shape. This can give people problems with their sight. Using the words from the WORD BANK, label the eyes below.

- lens
- nearsighted vision
- retina
- corrected nearsighted vision
- concave lens
- normal vision
- farsighted vision
- corrected farsighted vision
- convex lens

WORD BANK

normal vision	nearsighted vision
farsighted vision	corrected nearsighted vision
corrected farsighted vision	convex lens
concave lens	retina
lens	

Page 68

The Human Body IF8754   119   © 1990 Instructional Fair, Inc.

Answer Key

Sensational!
(Ear and Eye Review)

Name _____

Use the Word Bank to complete the puzzle.

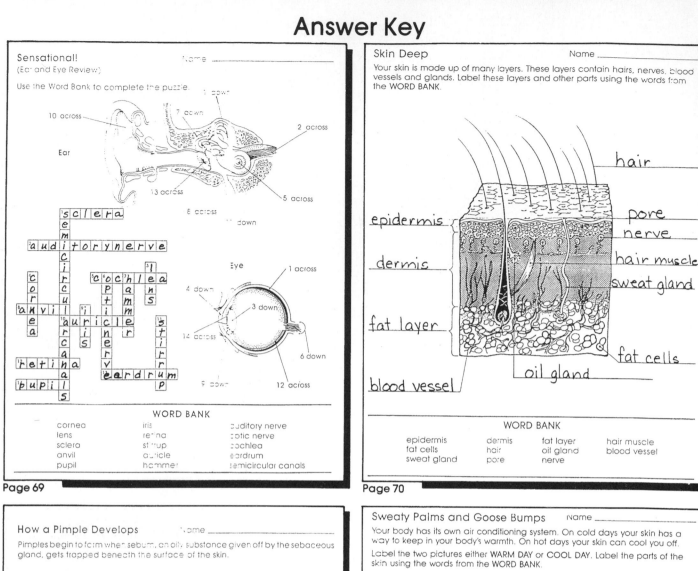

Ear

Eye

Crossword answers:
- sclera
- semicircular
- auditorynerve
- cochlea
- cornea
- optic
- anvil
- hammer
- auricle
- iris
- stirrup
- retina
- eardrum
- pupil

WORD BANK

cornea	iris	auditory nerve
lens	retina	optic nerve
sclera	stirrup	cochlea
anvil	auricle	eardrum
pupil	hammer	semicircular canals

Page 69

Skin Deep

Name _____

Your skin is made up of many layers. These layers contain hairs, nerves, blood vessels and glands. Label these layers and other parts using the words from the WORD BANK.

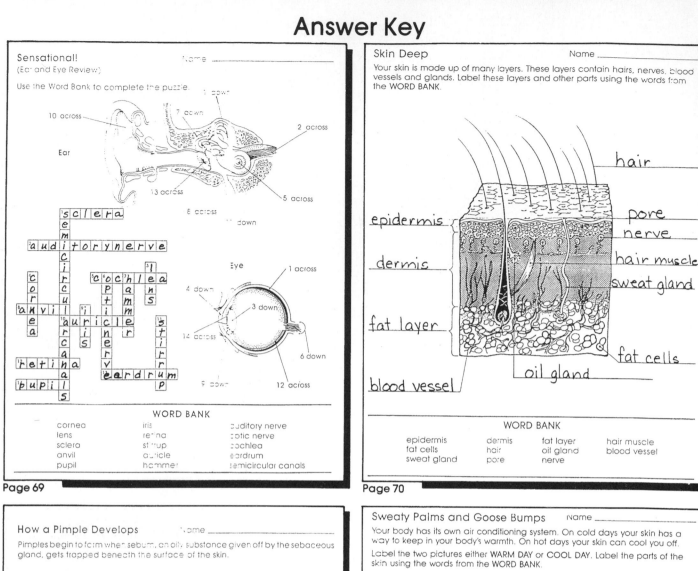

Labels: hair, epidermis, pore, nerve, dermis, hair muscle, sweat gland, fat layer, fat cells, blood vessel, oil gland

WORD BANK

epidermis	dermis	fat layer	hair muscle
fat cells	hair	oil gland	blood vessel
sweat gland	pore	nerve	

Page 70

How a Pimple Develops

Name _____

Pimples begin to form when sebum, an oily substance given off by the sebaceous gland, gets trapped beneath the surface of the skin.

Number the three stages pictured below. Label the parts illustrated in each stage.

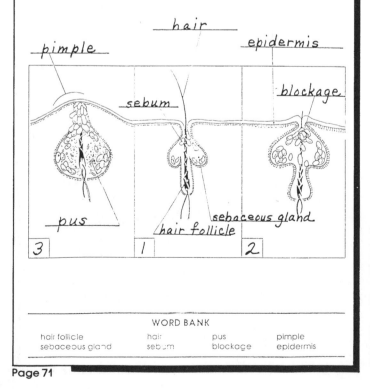

Labels: pimple, hair, epidermis, sebum, blockage, pus, sebaceous gland, hair follicle

Stages numbered: 3, 1, 2

WORD BANK

hair follicle	hair	pus	pimple
sebaceous gland	sebum	blockage	epidermis

Page 71

Sweaty Palms and Goose Bumps

Name _____

Your body has its own air conditioning system. On cold days your skin has a way to keep in your body's warmth. On hot days your skin can cool you off.

Label the two pictures either WARM DAY or COOL DAY. Label the parts of the skin using the words from the WORD BANK.

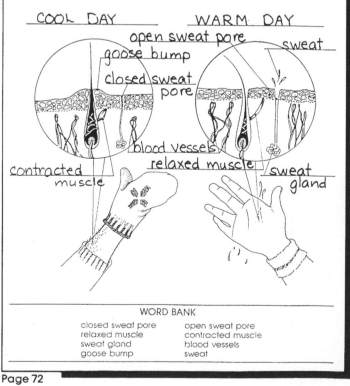

COOL DAY — goose bump, closed sweat pore, contracted muscle, blood vessels

WARM DAY — open sweat pore, sweat, relaxed muscle, sweat gland

WORD BANK

closed sweat pore	open sweat pore
relaxed muscle	contracted muscle
sweat gland	blood vessels
goose bump	sweat

Page 72

The Human Body IF8754   120

Answer Key

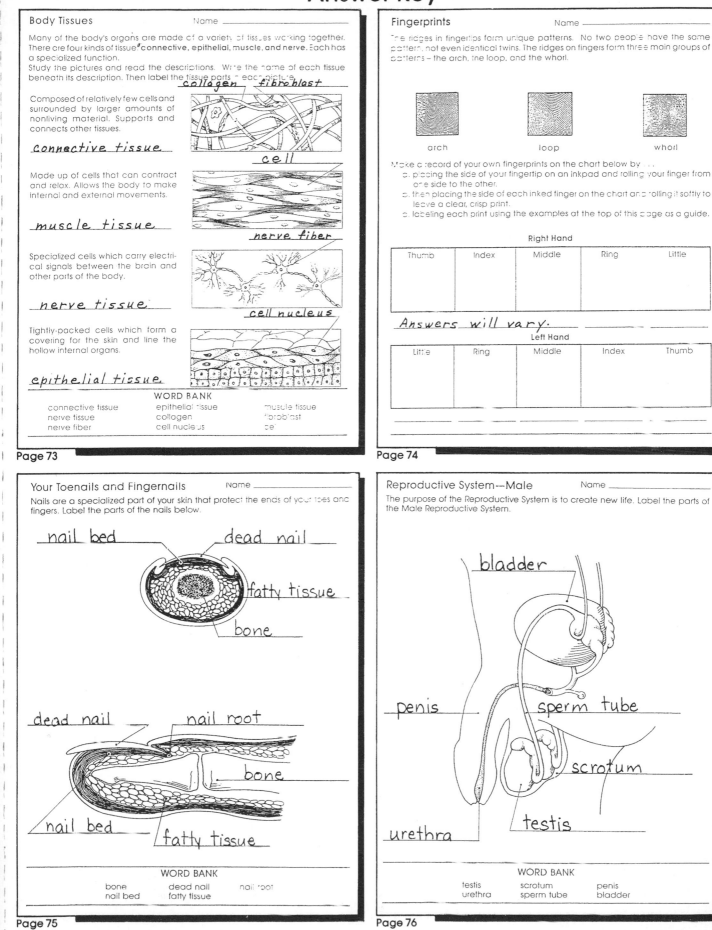

Body Tissues

Name _____

Many of the body's organs are made of a variety of tissues working together. There are four kinds of tissue: connective, epithelial, muscle, and nerve. Each has a specialized function.

Study the pictures and read the descriptions. Write the name of each tissue beneath its description. Then label the tissue parts in each picture.

collagen   fibroblast

Composed of relatively few cells and surrounded by larger amounts of nonliving material. Supports and connects other tissues.

connective tissue

cell

Made up of cells that can contract and relax. Allows the body to make internal and external movements.

muscle tissue

nerve fiber

Specialized cells which carry electrical signals between the brain and other parts of the body.

nerve tissue

cell nucleus

Tightly-packed cells which form a covering for the skin and line the hollow internal organs.

epithelial tissue

WORD BANK
connective tissue	epithelial tissue	muscle tissue
nerve tissue	collagen	fibroblast
nerve fiber	cell nucleus	cell

Fingerprints

Name _____

The ridges in fingertips form unique patterns. No two people have the same pattern, not even identical twins. The ridges on fingers form three main groups of patterns – the arch, the loop, and the whorl.

arch   loop   whorl

Make a record of your own fingerprints on the chart below by . . .
  a. placing the side of your fingertip on an inkpad and rolling your finger from one side to the other.
  b. then placing the side of each inked finger on the chart and rolling it softly to leave a clear, crisp print.
  c. labeling each print using the examples at the top of this page as a guide.

Right Hand

Thumb	Index	Middle	Ring	Little

Answers will vary.

Left Hand

Little	Ring	Middle	Index	Thumb

Your Toenails and Fingernails

Name _____

Nails are a specialized part of your skin that protect the ends of your toes and fingers. Label the parts of the nails below.

nail bed   dead nail

fatty tissue

bone

dead nail   nail root

bone

nail bed   fatty tissue

WORD BANK
bone	dead nail	nail root
nail bed	fatty tissue	

Reproductive System--Male

Name _____

The purpose of the Reproductive System is to create new life. Label the parts of the Male Reproductive System.

bladder

penis   sperm tube

scrotum

urethra   testis

WORD BANK
testis	scrotum	penis
urethra	sperm tube	bladder

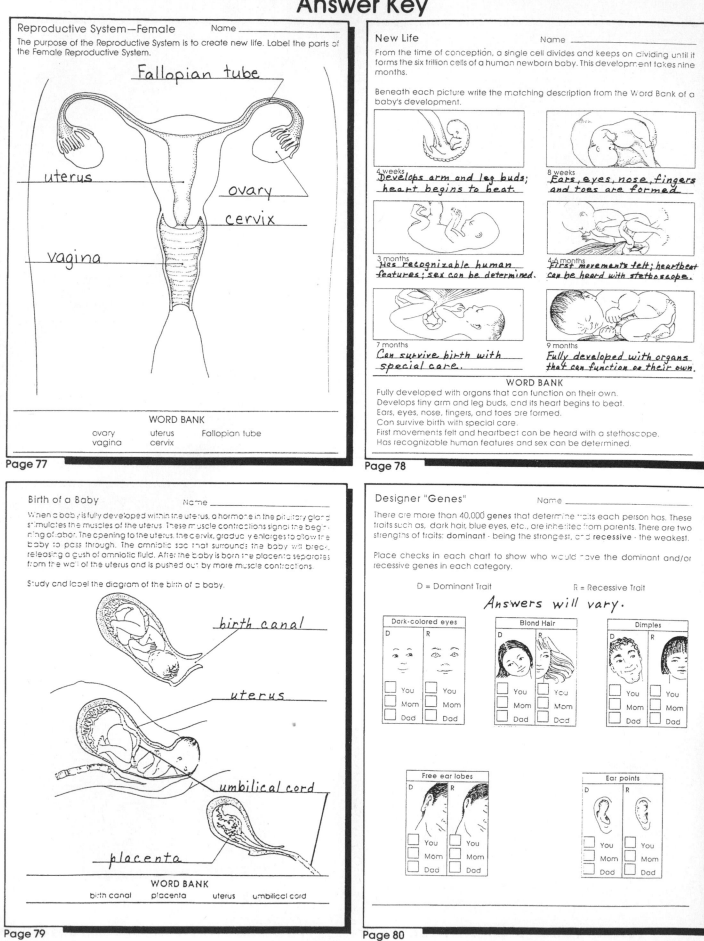

Reproductive System—Female

Name _____

The purpose of the Reproductive System is to create new life. Label the parts of the Female Reproductive System.

Fallopian tube

uterus

ovary

cervix

vagina

WORD BANK
ovary   uterus   Fallopian tube
vagina   cervix

Page 77

New Life

Name _____

From the time of conception, a single cell divides and keeps on dividing until it forms the six trillion cells of a human newborn baby. This development takes nine months.

Beneath each picture write the matching description from the Word Bank of a baby's development.

4 weeks — *Develops arm and leg buds; heart begins to beat.*

8 weeks — *Ears, eyes, nose, fingers and toes are formed.*

3 months — *Has recognizable human features; sex can be determined.*

4-6 months — *First movements felt; heartbeat can be heard with stethoscope.*

7 months — *Can survive birth with special care.*

9 months — *Fully developed with organs that can function on their own.*

WORD BANK
Fully developed with organs that can function on their own.
Develops tiny arm and leg buds, and its heart begins to beat.
Ears, eyes, nose, fingers, and toes are formed.
Can survive birth with special care.
First movements felt and heartbeat can be heard with a stethoscope.
Has recognizable human features and sex can be determined.

Page 78

Birth of a Baby

Name _____

When a baby is fully developed within the uterus, a hormone in the pituitary gland stimulates the muscles of the uterus. These muscle contractions signal the beginning of labor. The opening to the uterus, the cervix, gradually enlarges to allow the baby to pass through. The amniotic sac that surrounds the baby will break, releasing a gush of amniotic fluid. After the baby is born the placenta separates from the wall of the uterus and is pushed out by more muscle contractions.

Study and label the diagram of the birth of a baby.

birth canal

uterus

umbilical cord

placenta

WORD BANK
birth canal   placenta   uterus   umbilical cord

Page 79

Designer "Genes"

Name _____

There are more than 40,000 **genes** that determine traits each person has. These traits such as, dark hair, blue eyes, etc., are inherited from parents. There are two strengths of traits: **dominant** - being the strongest, and **recessive** - the weakest.

Place checks in each chart to show who would have the dominant and/or recessive genes in each category.

D = Dominant Trait   R = Recessive Trait

Answers will vary.

Dark-colored eyes
D	R
You	You
Mom	Mom
Dad	Dad

Blond Hair
D	R
You	You
Mom	Mom
Dad	Dad

Dimples
D	R
You	You
Mom	Mom
Dad	Dad

Free ear lobes
D	R
You	You
Mom	Mom
Dad	Dad

Ear points
D	R
You	You
Mom	Mom
Dad	Dad

Page 80

Answer Key

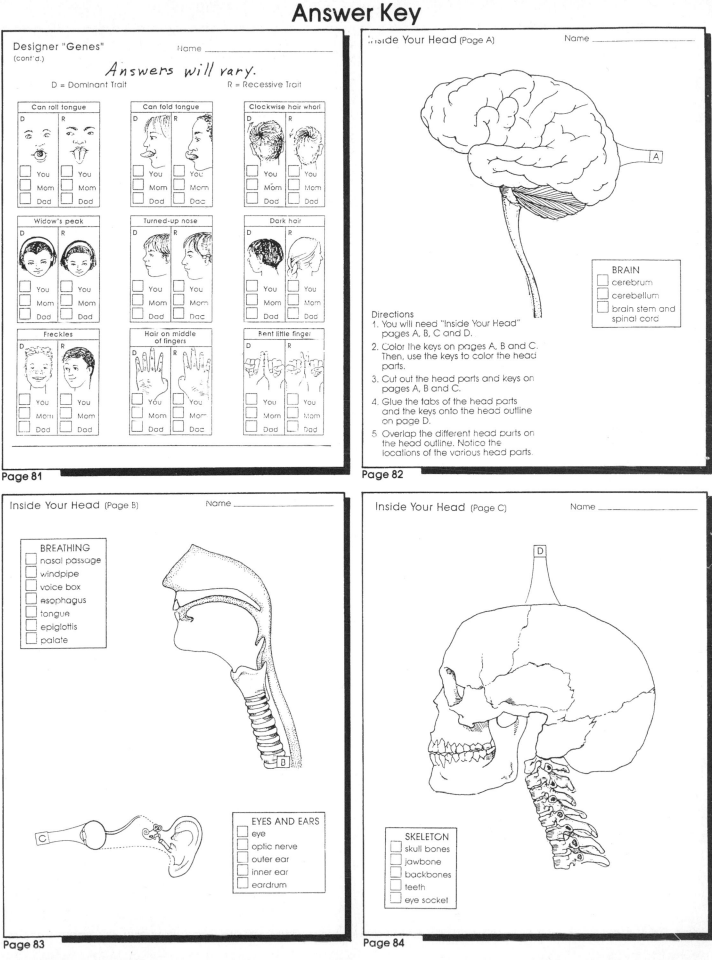

Designer "Genes" (cont'd.)

Name _____

Answers will vary.

D = Dominant Trait   R = Recessive Trait

Can roll tongue

D	R
☐ You	☐ You
☐ Mom	☐ Mom
☐ Dad	☐ Dad

Can fold tongue

D	R
☐ You	☐ You
☐ Mom	☐ Mom
☐ Dad	☐ Dad

Clockwise hair whorl

D	R
☐ You	☐ You
☐ Mom	☐ Mom
☐ Dad	☐ Dad

Widow's peak

D	R
☐ You	☐ You
☐ Mom	☐ Mom
☐ Dad	☐ Dad

Turned-up nose

D	R
☐ You	☐ You
☐ Mom	☐ Mom
☐ Dad	☐ Dad

Dark hair

D	R
☐ You	☐ You
☐ Mom	☐ Mom
☐ Dad	☐ Dad

Freckles

D	R
☐ You	☐ You
☐ Mom	☐ Mom
☐ Dad	☐ Dad

Hair on middle of fingers

D	R
☐ You	☐ You
☐ Mom	☐ Mom
☐ Dad	☐ Dad

Bent little finger

D	R
☐ You	☐ You
☐ Mom	☐ Mom
☐ Dad	☐ Dad

Page 81

Inside Your Head (Page A)

Name _____

☐ **BRAIN**
☐ cerebrum
☐ cerebellum
☐ brain stem and spinal cord

Directions

1. You will need "Inside Your Head" pages A, B, C and D.
2. Color the keys on pages A, B and C. Then, use the keys to color the head parts.
3. Cut out the head parts and keys on pages A, B and C.
4. Glue the tabs of the head parts and the keys onto the head outline on page D.
5. Overlap the different head parts on the head outline. Notice the locations of the various head parts.

Page 82

Inside Your Head (Page B)

Name _____

☐ **BREATHING**
☐ nasal passage
☐ windpipe
☐ voice box
☐ esophagus
☐ tongue
☐ epiglottis
☐ palate

☐ **EYES AND EARS**
☐ eye
☐ optic nerve
☐ outer ear
☐ inner ear
☐ eardrum

Page 83

Inside Your Head (Page C)

Name _____

☐ **SKELETON**
☐ skull bones
☐ jawbone
☐ backbones
☐ teeth
☐ eye socket

Page 84

The Human Body IF8754   123   © 1990 Instructional Fair, Inc.

Answer Key

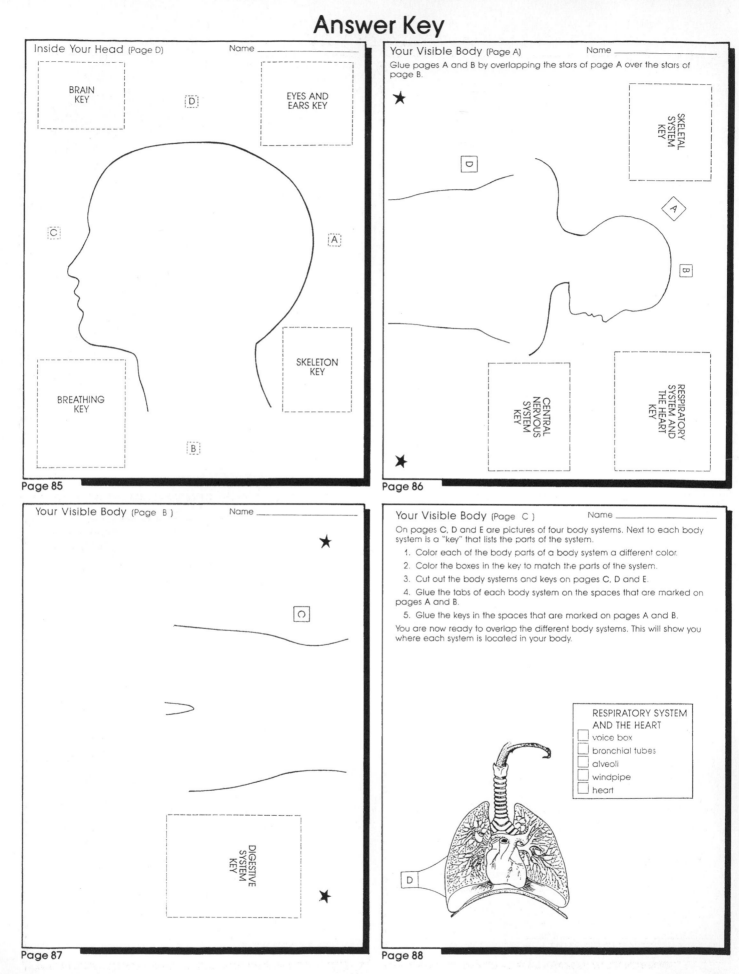

Inside Your Head (Page D)   Name _____

BRAIN
KEY

D

EYES AND
EARS KEY

C

A

SKELETON
KEY

BREATHING
KEY

B

Page 85

Your Visible Body (Page A)   Name _____

Glue pages A and B by overlapping the stars of page A over the stars of page B.

★

SKELETAL
SYSTEM
KEY

D

A

B

CENTRAL
NERVOUS
SYSTEM
KEY

RESPIRATORY
SYSTEM AND
THE HEART
KEY

★

Page 86

Your Visible Body (Page B)   Name _____

★

C

DIGESTIVE
SYSTEM
KEY

★

Page 87

Your Visible Body (Page C)   Name _____

On pages C, D and E are pictures of four body systems. Next to each body system is a "key" that lists the parts of the system.

1. Color each of the body parts of a body system a different color.

2. Color the boxes in the key to match the parts of the system.

3. Cut out the body systems and keys on pages C, D and E.

4. Glue the tabs of each body system on the spaces that are marked on pages A and B.

5. Glue the keys in the spaces that are marked on pages A and B.

You are now ready to overlap the different body systems. This will show you where each system is located in your body.

RESPIRATORY SYSTEM
AND THE HEART
☐ voice box
☐ bronchial tubes
☐ alveoli
☐ windpipe
☐ heart

D

Page 88

Answer Key

Your Visible Body (Page D)

SKELETAL SYSTEM
- [ ] backbone
- [ ] ribs
- [ ] skull
- [ ] breastbone
- [ ] hipbone

A

Your Visible Body (Page E)

B

DIGESTIVE SYSTEM
- [ ] saliva glands
- [ ] esophagus
- [ ] stomach
- [ ] liver
- [ ] pancreas
- [ ] gall bladder
- [ ] large intestine
- [ ] small intestine
- [ ] appendix

C

CENTRAL NERVOUS SYSTEM
- [ ] cerebrum
- [ ] cerebellum
- [ ] medulla
- [ ] spinal cord

Organ Systems

Name _____

Make an "X" in the correct box to show to which system/systems each organ belongs. One is done for you.

Organs	Systems						
	Digestive	Respiratory	Urinary	Reproductive	Circulatory	Nervous	Endocrine
Bladder			X				
Brain						X	
Heart					X		
Ovaries				X			X
Liver	X						
Pancreas	X						X
Kidneys			X				
Spinal Cord						X	
Lungs		X					
Small Intestines	X						
Diaphragm		X					
Mouth	X	X					
Nerves						X	
Testes				X			X
Thyroid Gland							X
Arteries			X		X		
Esophagus	X						
Cerebellum						X	

Think Fast!

Name _____

The time it takes for your ears to send a message to your brain, and your body to respond is called **reaction time**.

Let's try an experiment to test your reaction time.

Materials: 30 cm metric ruler.

Procedure:

1. Place your left arm on a table with your hand over the edge.

2. Space your thumb and index fingers about 4 cm apart.

3. Have a partner hold the "30 cm end" of the ruler, with the other end just above your open thumb and index finger.

4. Your partner will say "set," and drop the ruler.

5. Catch the ruler with your thumb and index finger as quickly as possible.

6. Check the distance fallen by taking a reading at the bottom of the index finger.

7. Record your results.

8. Repeat the procedure 10 times with each hand.

Are you right-handed, or left-handed? Which of your hands was the quickest?

Did others find the same results?

_____

Trial #	Reaction Distance	
	Left Hand	Right Hand
1.	*Answers*	
2.	*will vary.*	
3.		
4.		
5.		
6.		
7.		
8.		
9.		
10.		

Answer Key

Feel the Beat

Name _____

When the heart pumps, it forces blood out into the arteries. The walls of the arteries expand and contract to the rhythm of the heart which creates a **pulse**.

You can feel your pulse where the arteries are close to the surface of the skin. Two good places to feel a pulse are on the inside of the wrist, and on the neck to the side of the windpipe.

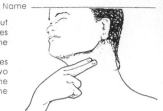

The type of activity you are doing can greatly affect the rate of your pulse. Try the experiments below and complete the chart by –
1. counting the number of heart beats in 15 seconds.
2. multiplying that number by 4 to get the pulse rate for one minute.

Study your results. Explain how each type of activity affected your pulse rate. *Answers will vary.*

Activity	Pulse Rate for 15 sec.	X 4 =	Pulse Rate per minute
Sitting still for 10 minutes.			
Running in place for 3 minutes.			
Just after finishing your lunch or dinner.			
While still in bed in the morning.			
Just after getting ready for school.			

Pressure Points

Name _____

When a person is severely cut and begins to bleed, it's time for quick action. First aid for severe bleeding involves applying pressure over the wound. Sometimes it is possible to press the artery above the wound against the bone behind it, and stop the bleeding. This place is called a **pressure point**. A pressure point is also an excellent location to take a person's pulse.

Place an "X" on the pressure points listed in the Word Bank.

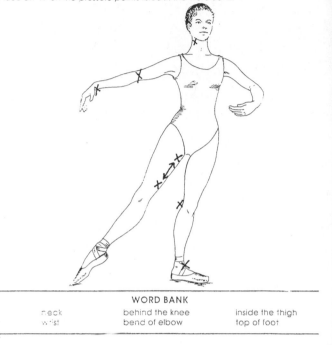

WORD BANK

neck	behind the knee	inside the thigh
wrist	bend of elbow	top of foot

Food Pyramid

Name _____

Your body will get the nutrients it needs if you follow the rules of the food group pyramid. Be sure to make fruits, vegetables, and grains the basic foods of your diet. Eat plenty of healthy foods from the bottom of the pyramid every day.

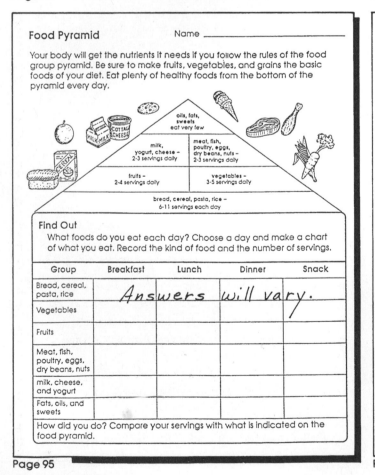

oils, fats, sweets eat very few

milk, yogurt, cheese – 2-3 servings daily

meat, fish, poultry, eggs, dry beans, nuts – 2-3 servings daily

fruits – 2-4 servings daily

vegetables – 3-5 servings daily

bread, cereal, pasta, rice – 6-11 servings each day

Find Out

What foods do you eat each day? Choose a day and make a chart of what you eat. Record the kind of food and the number of servings.

Group	Breakfast	Lunch	Dinner	Snack
Bread, cereal, pasta, rice	*Answers*	*will*	*vary.*	
Vegetables				
Fruits				
Meat, fish, poultry, eggs, dry beans, nuts				
milk, cheese, and yogurt				
Fats, oils, and sweets				

How did you do? Compare your servings with what is indicated on the food pyramid.

Snacker's Survey

Name _____

Do you have a bad case of the munchies, crunchies, or nibbles? Some snack foods can be good for you, while others are terrible. Foods that are lower on the food pyramid are usually much better for you because they contain smaller amounts of fat.

Take a **Snacker's Survey**.

fats, oils, sweets

milk, yogurt, cheese

meat, fish, poultry, eggs, dry beans, nuts

fruits | vegetables

bread, cereal, pasta, rice

Snacker's Survey

Write the food group to which each snack belongs. Then, using a scale of 1-10, with 1 being the lowest, give each snack a taste score and a nutrition score.

Snack	Food Group	Taste Score	Nutrition Score
Apple	fruits	Answers	
Cheese	dairy	will	
Cookie	sweets	vary.	
Potato Chips	bread oils		
Orange	fruits		
Carrot	vegetables		
Cake	sweets		
Candy Bar	sweets		
Bagel	grains		
Beef Jerky	fats meats		
Popcorn	grains		
Pretzels	bread		

Fun Fact!

Labels might not use the name sugar when it lists a sweetener. Watch for other names for sugar.

Dextrose	Lactose
Corn Syrup	Fructose
Molasses	Sucrose

Answer Key

Name the Nutrient

Name _____

Your body is made up of millions of cells that need food to stay alive. Your body needs nutrients from the foods you eat to help the cells grow and repair themselves. Nutrients are divided into six major groups: fats, proteins, carbohydrates, minerals, vitamins and water.

Read each clue. Identify the nutrient.

"I'm the body's building material. You need me to make new tissue. You get plenty of me from milk, beans, meat, and peanuts."
Who am I? **protein**

"I give you energy to work and play. You can find me in starchy foods like pasta and potatoes."
Who am I? **carbohydrate**

"I help build strong bones and teeth. I also give you healthy red blood. You can find me in all four food groups."
Who am I? **mineral**

"I give you a concentrated source of energy. You can find me in oily and greasy foods, like bacon, salad dressing, and butter. I also help you maintain healthy skin and hair."
Who am I? **fat**

"You might call me the alphabet soup of the nutrients. I am one of the essential nutrients. I don't give you energy, but I do help your body get energy from the other nutrients."
Who am I? **vitamin**

"I make up over half of your body weight. My job is to carry all those good nutrients throughout your body. I also help your body to remove wastes."
Who am I? **water**

WORD BANK
fat
protein
carbohydrate
water
vitamin
mineral

You Are What You Eat

Name _____

Looking closely at the information on a cereal box you can learn many interesting things about the product.

Carefully read the information on the illustration of the cereal box. Answer the questions. Compare these answers with the information found on a box of cereal you might eat for breakfast.

	Corn Balls	Your Cereal
What kind of grain(s) is used?	corn	Answers will vary.
Is sugar used?	yes	
What position is sugar on the list of ingredients?	2nd	
List other sweeteners.	corn syrup molasses	
How many calories per serving without milk?	110	
How many calories per per serving when eaten with 1/2 cup of skim milk?	150	
How much protein per serving?	1g	
How many vitamins and minerals does the cereal contain?	10	
How much cholesterol is in one serving?	0 mg	
How much fat is in one serving?	0 g	
How much carbohydrate is in one serving?	26 g	

Burning Calories to Stay Healthy

Name _____

Regular exercise makes your heart strong, and it also helps you burn calories so you maintain a healthy weight.

The activities named below list the number of calories burned by a 150-pound person when he or she engages in an activity for 30 minutes. Circle the 10 activities below that help you burn the most calories.

Activity	Calories Burned in 30 Minutes	Activity	Calories Burned in 30 Minutes
cross country skiing	210	homework	55
running (7 mph)	275	racquetball	365
shuffleboard	90	baseball	60
bicycling (stationary)	150	soccer	360
aerobic dancing	200	swimming	265
watching TV	45	tennis	225
walking (5.5 mph)	280	basketball	345

Complete the chart below to keep a record of the exercise you do for one week.

	Type of Exercise	Length of Time (minutes)	Approximate Calories Burned
Sunday	Answers will vary.		
Monday			
Tuesday			
Wednesday			
Thursday			
Friday			
Saturday			

Reading the Label

Name _____

The labels on medicine containers give us important information. Labels should always be read carefully.

Read the information on the cough medicine labels below. Answer the questions on the lines provided.

6-Hour Cough Relief
Fast, effective relief for coughs due to colds and flu.

Recommended Dosage:
Children (5 - 12 years): 1 teaspoon every 6 hours.
Adults: 2 teaspoons every 6 hours.
Caution: *Do not administer to children under 5. No more than 4 dosages per day. This product may cause drowsiness; use caution if operating machinery or driving a vehicle. Should not be taken if you are pregnant or nursing a child.*
If cough or fever persists, consult a physician.
Exp. Date: 8/93

1. What is the adult dosage? **2 teas. every 6 hours**

2. What is a child's dosage? **1 teas. every 6 hours**

3. What is a side effect of this medicine? **drowsiness**

4. Who should not take this medicine? **child under 5; pregnant or nursing mother**

5. How many dosages per day can be taken safely? **4**

6. What is the expiration date of this medicine? **August, 1993**

7. What action should be taken if the medicine does not relieve your cough?
Consult your physician

8. For what symptoms should this medicine be taken?
Coughs due to colds and flu

Answer Key

Caution: Poison!   Name _____

Children are always very curious. They love to touch things and pick them up. Very young children like to put things into their mouths. What action do you take if a child swallows a poisonous material?

Read the following safety procedures.

CALL YOUR POISON CONTROL CENTER, HOSPITAL, PHYSICIAN, OR EMERGENCY PHONE NUMBER IMMEDIATELY!!

If you cannot obtain emergency advice, follow these procedures.

• If the poison is **corrosive**: paint remover, household cleaners, gasoline, drain opener, ammonia or lye, **DO NOT** make the patient vomit. Give the patient water or milk to dilute the poison.

• If the poison is **not corrosive**: insect spray, aspirin, pesticides or medicine, **make the patient vomit**, or use a poison control kit. To force the patient to vomit touch the back of his/her throat.

Write a bold "V" on each picture that shows poison that should be vomited if swallowed. **Circle** each poison that should **not** be vomited if swallowed.

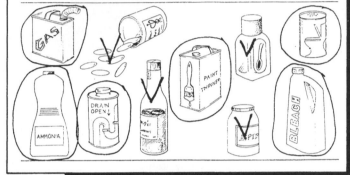

Human Body Review   Name _____

Use the Word Bank to complete the puzzle.

Across:
1. outer layer of skin
4. the blood pump
6. stores urine
10. the "bite" is the _____ of the teeth
11. opening to the uterus
12. boney structure
13. the inside of the hand
14. controls body growth and other glands
17. a break in a bone
20. rhythm of the heart creates a _____
21. female sex glands
22. determine human traits

Down:
1. waste removal system
2. outer layer of the tooth
3. upper arm bone
5. gland that goes to work when we are excited, angry, or frightened
7. fluid surrounding fetus
8. long food tube
9. joint found in elbow
12. oily substance given off by the sebaceous gland
13. gland which controls the body's use of glucose
15. place by or beside a wound to stop bleeding
16. muscles are attached to the skeleton by _____
18. male sex glands
19. framework of bones that supports lower part of abdomen

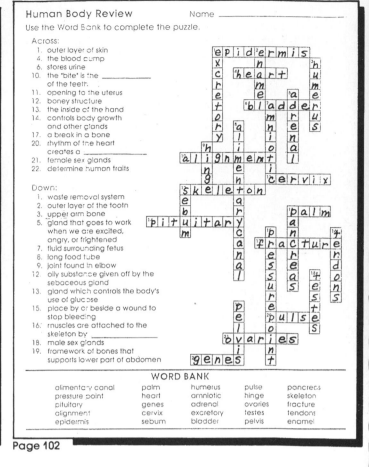

WORD BANK

alimentary canal	palm	humerus	pulse	pancreas
pressure point	heart	amniotic	hinge	skeleton
pituitary	genes	adrenal	ovaries	fracture
alignment	cervix	excretory	testes	tendons
epidermis	sebum	bladder	pelvis	enamel